fried
chicken

AN AMERICAN STORY

fried chicken

AN AMERICAN STORY

John T. Edge

G. P. PUTNAM'S SONS
NEW YORK

The recipes contained in this book are to be followed exactly as written. The Publisher is not responsible for specific health or allergy needs that may require medical supervision. The Publisher is not responsible for any adverse reactions to the recipes contained in this book.

G. P. Putnam's Sons
Publishers Since 1838
a member of
Penguin Group (USA) Inc.
375 Hudson Street
New York, NY 10014

Photographs of Mattie Smith, Greenwood, Mississippi (p. viii), and of Jesse Clifton Evans Edge (p. 182) © Amy Evans
Lyrics to "Fried Chicken and a Country Tune" (p. 65) by C. Harwell

Library of Congress Cataloging-in-Publication Data

Edge, John T., date.
Fried chicken : an American story / John T. Edge.
p.   cm.
ISBN 0-399-15183-4
1. Cookery (Chicken).   2. Fried food.   I. Title.
TX750.5.C45E35   2004   2004044499
641.6'65—dc22

Printed in the United States of America
1   3   5   7   9   10   8   6   4   2

This book is printed on acid-free paper. ∞

Book design by Stephanie Huntwork

FOR MY SON, JESSE CLIFTON EVANS EDGE.
MAY YOU NEVER KNOW A McNUGGET.

i t is possible that anyone claiming to be considered an educated gentleman may be thought to have done a bold thing in publishing a book on poultry, and giving his real name on the title page.

Treatise on the History and Management
of Ornamental and Domestic Poultry (1849)
—REVEREND EDMUND SAUL DIXON

Contents

Introduction

This is the first in a series of books that celebrates America's iconic foods. Fried chicken leads off, then in quick succession come apple pie, donuts, hamburgers & french fries. To my mind, these are democratic foods that conjure our collective childhood and call to mind the question once posed by a Chinese philosopher: "What is patriotism, but nostalgia for the foods of our youth?"

I chose these foods because they transcend inter-regional variation and internecine debate over origins. Recognized from the Atlantic to the Pacific as uniquely American, they evoke the culinary and cultural fabric of our nation.

Though the places profiled and the recipes detailed can be read as keys to eating well here in the States, my intent was not to compile a list of the country's top spots. Instead, please consider this work to be my pilgrimage in search of America's greasy grail. In this book and the ones that follow, I strive to introduce you to people and foods that, by virtue of their myriad ethnicities, by dint of their unvarnished honesty, comprise a tapestry of America.

ONE

Wherein I Argue for
a New Theory
of Fried Chicken

fried chicken is best served without a side
of provincial bluster. I trace that realization to an encounter with Jim Villas's 1982
book, *American Taste*. The North Carolinian observed, "Let's not beat around the bush for
one second. To know about fried chicken, you
have to have been weaned and reared on it in
the South. Period."

As a fellow weaned and reared Southerner,
I initially embraced Villas's pronouncement.
But more recently, while spending a year on

the road in search of America by way of fried chicken, I've learned that Villas was wrong. Eating my way across the girth of our nation, I found much evidence to support the notion that, though the South has a long and distinguished history of fried chicken cookery, we have no lock on excellence.

No palate can deny the appeal of the bread-crumb-coated chicken backs I gnawed in Barberton, Ohio; or the mojo-marinated breasts I devoured in Miami; or the cornmeal-crusted drumsticks I savored in Seattle. The notion that Southerners have an exclusive on fried chicken is attributable to an enduring phenomenon, the blind ascription to Southern distinctiveness. You know the routine: Summers are muggier, girls are prettier, dogs are lazier way down south in Dixie. A while back, I read an essay wherein an academic argues that the South is not necessarily richer in history or tradition or memories, but that owing to its peculiar past, the region plows more of its intellectual energy into telling tales that are at best playfully boastful, at worst, self-aggrandizing. Tales like, "To know about fried chicken, you have to have been weaned and reared on it in the South. Period."

I'm not one to abjure my native victuals. I own three cast-iron skillets. Each, by way of repeated use, is burnished black as Satan's bung. I am adept at rendering lard, and I dote on the cracklings that sink to the bottom. I've yet to eat my fill of chicken fried in the Southern manner; I can hold forth with the best of my kinsmen as to proper preparation and consumption.

But bad comes with good. As a Southerner, I also find it

difficult to wash my palate clear of the bitter taint of racism. Herein, I pay homage to the region's legendary fry cooks of African descent. To do so is to document the sad injustices of a Jim Crow South where blacks worked in white homes and businesses, wringing chicken necks and hefting skillets to stovetops, but were denied a place at the lunch counter, the dining room table.

I tell some Southern stories in the pages that follow. But education is funny. Expose a boy to the wide world, and soon he develops a heretical idea or two. As in, "Fried chicken is not distinctly Southern; maybe it's not even distinctly American." Or, better yet, "If fried chicken is American, then it denotes an American identity that accommodates cooks from a plethora of traditions."

a case in point: Many of the cooks I've met lately have been recent immigrants who, intent upon assimilation, fry chicken in a conscious attempt to cook an iconically American dish. And yet, a glimmer of home oftentimes shines through. The effect is not diverting so much as it is mosaic-making. Legions of Korean entrepreneurs fit this pattern, including the interrelated Baltimore purveyors—at Lexington Fried Chicken, Park's Fried Chicken, and Super Fried Chicken—who, in addition to fried breasts and wings and drumsticks, sell fried chicken necks and fried rice.

Other entrepreneurs further complicate the equation. At New Caporal in New York City, Dominican fry cooks serve

Cuban-inflected orange-garlic-and-lime-marinated chicken to a mostly African American clientele. Thirty blocks away at El Mundo, their countrymen dole out vinegar-marinated chicken to a mostly Dominican crowd that, for the most part, forsakes the chicken in favor of a smashed plantain and pork dish known as mofongo.

S pend a year eating fried chicken, inhaling fried chicken fumes day and night, and just at the point when you're about to go bonkers, everything comes into focus. Somewhere along the way, maybe while munching a three-buck bag of *chicharrones de pollo* from El Mundo, I experienced such an epiphany. I had always known that, to understand chicken as fried in these United States, I would have to deal with more than the Southern question; I would have to contend with the matter of mystique. And in order to be well equipped to do so, I spent an inordinate amount of time collecting fried chicken lore.

I knew the basics: that the Depression-era Republican Party slogan "A chicken in every pot" was derivative of a pledge made by King Henri IV of France, who in the sixteenth century pronounced, "I hope to make France so prosperous that every peasant will have a chicken in his pot on Sundays." And I knew that such statements packed wallops because, until the latter half of the twentieth century, chickens were expensive. That's expensive as in costing more than beef, more than veal.

I knew that the relatively sudden transition from luxury to

commodity animated our conflicted love affair with fried chicken, that the transition could explain our tendency to sentimentalize the dish, to cloak it in family and home, though devotees are not above digging into an eight-piece box from Popeye's. Therein I gleaned a defining paradox: Fried chicken is at once a totem of tradition and a lowest-common-denominator lunch.

What's more, fried chicken is the stuff of song, as in "Fried Chicken," a single cut in 1957 by Hank Penny, that featured a song called "Rock of Gibraltar" on the B-side. Not to mention the musical stylings of a guitar virtuoso named Buckethead who won fame by wearing a KFC bucket for a crown and claiming that he was raised in a chicken coop. "One night, a guy threw a bucket of chicken into the coop," a Buckethead spokesperson explained in a 1999 newspaper article. "Buckethead freaked out and tried to put the chickens back together. Then he stuck the bucket on his head. By doing that, he got the power of the dead chickens."

Fried chicken is also the stuff of pathos. "When I was three and Bailey was four, we had arrived in the musty little town, wearing tags on our wrists which instructed that we were Marguerite and Bailey Johnson, Jr., from Long Beach, California, en route to Stamps, Arkansas," wrote Maya Angelou in her memoir *I Know Why the Caged Bird Sings*. "Our parents had decided to put an end to their calamitous marriage, and father shipped us home to his mother. A [railroad] porter had been charged with our welfare . . . and our tickets were pinned to my brother's inside coat pocket. I don't remember much of the trip, but after we reached the segregated southern part of the journey, things must have looked up. Negro passengers, who always traveled with loaded lunch boxes, felt sorry for the 'poor, motherless darlings' and plied us with cold fried chicken and potato salad."

Fried chicken is the stuff of tragicomedy. "Last time I was down South, I walked into this restaurant," wrote Dick Gregory in his memoir *Callus on My Soul.* "This white waitress came up to me and said, 'We don't serve colored people here.' I said, 'That's all right, I don't eat colored people. Bring me a whole fried chicken.' About that time, these three cousins came in. You know the ones I mean, Ku, Klux, and Klan. They said, 'Boy, we're givin' you fair warnin'. Anything you do to that chicken, we're gonna do to you.'

"So I put down my knife and picked up that chicken and kissed it."

You may read the pages that follow in a couple of different ways. Read the following chapters as a social history of modern America told by way of fried chicken, and hopefully you won't be disappointed. Or you might choose to eat your way through this text, to come to know the life stories of these American cooks by way of their good cooking, treating my observations as historical and cultural footnotes.

Either way, you will learn, among other things, how to

cook Italian fried chicken from a man born in India. You will make up your own mind about whether Kansas City can claim the title Pan-Fried Chicken Capital of America. You will taste Creole fried chicken in Louisiana, Buffalo fried chicken in upstate New York, and Latin fried chicken in California.

The first half of the book is dedicated, in large part, to my search for fried chicken in the margins, but you will also come to know revered traditional cooks like Deacon Lyndell Burton of Atlanta, who operated one of the early integrated lunch spots in the city; Hattie Edwards of Gordonsville, Virginia, who perpetuated the local tradition of meeting train passengers with platters of chicken and sleeves of deviled eggs; and Dot Burton and Lucille Thompson of the Chalfonte Hotel in Cape May, New Jersey, who, like their mother before them, claim more than fifty years at the stove.

And if I do my job well, you may be compelled to turn to the rear of each chapter and cook your way through the representative recipes I assembled. Some are of my own divination, as the original recipes were secret. Others were generously offered. Either way, they are a tribute to the good people who invited me to sit down at their table and trusted me with their life stories.

One more thing: You will find no nuggets here. No chicken fingers either. By my reckoning, fried chicken must have a bone. I have spent many hours contemplating the question of what qualifies as true fried chicken. My chosen place to ponder this matter was the Chevron mini-mart, three blocks from my home in Oxford, Mississippi. Contrary to what the cashier might have concluded, I was not wasting the night away, sipping absently from a cup of coffee, but formulating a theory of fried chicken that would exclude all manner of fused chicken parts.

My neighborhood Chevron was the ideal laboratory. Though there are two other Chevrons in downtown Oxford, the one on my street corner is known as the Chicken-on-a-Stick Chevron because, soon after the bars close and the fraternity socials peter out, the undergraduate demimonde descends upon *this* mini-mart, in search of sustenance of the fowl sort: die-cut chicken parts, breaded and threaded on pointy wooden skewers, and deep-fried to a sandy brown. I have been known to stumble home from a night on the town, clutching a bagful to my breast. That said, I have come to the conclusion—after intensive and sober study—that, although it may well be a close relative, chicken-on-a-stick does not fried chicken make.

Sure, one chicken-on-a-stick will take the edge off a six-pack buzz, but is it true fried chicken? Hardly. The presence of a bone in a piece of fried chicken is functionally and formally elemental. Without a bone, chicken lacks its savory essence, its primal, Henry VIII appeal. (The introduction of knives and forks to sixteenth-century Europe did not wholly sway lovers of poultry, who continue to savor birds out of hand.) And never mind the chicken-on-a-stick lovers who would argue that the wooden skewer serves as a proxy for a drumstick. By way of inelegant emulation, they prove my point.

TWO

Skillet Sisters
of the
Chalfonte Hotel

i n an effort to be true to my quest, regardless of relation to the line mapped by Mason and Dixon, our story begins in New Jersey, along the coast. Though the region appears to flourish, the true heyday hereabouts was the last half of the nineteenth century when this tongue of land, stretching southward from Atlantic City, was the playground of the elite and influential. Local wags like to say that Cape May, the village at the southernmost tip of the tongue, is America's oldest seaside resort.

Given half a chance they will tell you that President Abraham Lincoln made the journey to Cape May to escape the oppressive summer heat of miasmic Washington. One man, who misinterpreted my interest in local restaurant history to be applicable to all facets of Cape May lore, flagged me down in the parking lot of the visitor's center to inform me that Henry Ford raced prototype autos on the beaches here, besting all comers until he lost to a man named Chevrolet. But I didn't drive my rental car down from Newark to hear such stories. I came to eat fried chicken at the Chalfonte Hotel.

I arrive at the inn—a clapboard dowager embellished with Romeo and Juliet balconies—armed with a modicum of information. I know that Dot Burton and Lucille Thompson, the Chalfonte's long-tenured cooks, fry chicken in two gargantuan cast-iron skillets that are so large they accommodate twenty or thirty pieces at a time. And I soon come to know that locals like to tell tales about how those skillets have been in continual use since the days when Lincoln walked the beach.

Before even unpacking, I make for the kitchen. It's just past five on a summer afternoon, and, according to the desk clerk, "the ladies are pulling the last of the chicken from the skillets." Once escorted into the presence of Dot and Lucille, I ask a silly question: "Why do people come to the Chalfonte?" (I have a stunning facility for insightful question-making.)

Lucille laughs and turns the other way. Dot, who is spearing russet-hued pieces of chicken from a skillet the circumference of a manhole cover, looks me up and down and says, "Hell if I know. They don't have air-conditioning, don't have telephones or televisions in the little old rooms, and you have to walk down the hall just to use the bathroom." And then, as an impish grin steals across her face, she allows, "It might have something to do with the food."

dot Burton and Lucille Thompson learned to cook at the hem of their mother, Helen Dickerson, who, at the age of four, began her seventy-seven years of service at the Chalfonte. Her first job was flower girl, charged with gathering daisies and jonquils for the dinner table. Like their mother before them, these women have spent the great majority of their working lives at the Chalfonte. Dot began her tenure at the age of nine, washing sand from bathing suits and hanging the cleaned garments on guest doorknobs. Lucille came into the fold soon after, and save a period in the 1970s when she moved upstate to Princeton in a successful search for a husband, has been right by her sister's side.

Tight nests of gray curls frame their round faces. Dot and Lucille wear matching chef's whites, appreciate the balm of a good scotch, and share an unflagging devotion to the midday soap *Guiding Light.* You get the impression they might be twins, though Dot is seventy-six, Lucille seventy-five. They are both quick to laugh, and when they do, they cackle like schoolgirls. Among curators of Chalfonte lore, however, they are both considered more reserved than their mother: In her later years, Helen Dickerson took to holding court at a prep table, wagging her knife at passersby. If you dared enter the kitchen without greeting her by name, she was likely to fix you with an earnest gaze and ask, "Did I sleep with you last night?"

As young children Dot and Lucille shuttled back and forth from Richmond, Virginia, ancestral home of the Dickerson family, spending the school year in Virginia and Memorial Day to Columbus Day at Cape May. Accordingly, they claim a kind of divided loyalty, first to New Jersey, then to Virginia. But Dot—who, upon the death of their mother in 1990, assumed the job of Chalfonte fry cook—will tell you that, though the skillets are from Virginia, the recipe that her mother perfected came from a woman named Winifred Jones who hailed from Philadelphia, Pennsylvania.

Like many a closely guarded recipe, the secret to Chalfonte-style fried chicken is actually quite simple. (Consider KFC's famous eleven herbs and spices. When William Poundstone, author of the book *Big Secrets*, hired a laboratory to analyze KFC's famous seasoning mix, the results were a little shy of the Colonel's claim: flour, salt, pepper, and MSG.) At the Chalfonte, the trick is even simpler. For reasons that are unclear to Dot, the distinctive feature of their recipe involves tossing a heap of thickly sliced onions into the grease just before lowering the first batch of floured chicken. The onions will fry alongside the chicken, batch after batch, turning darker and darker until the shreds of onions resemble flue-cured tobacco leaves.

It's seven in the evening, before I head to the dining room, intent upon eating my fill of this deceptively simple fried chicken. I take a seat by a screened window, hoping that I'll catch a breeze. The dowdy old shotgun ballroom is about half full. Wood flooring creaks beneath the trod of the college kids who work summers as waiters. Fans suspended from the eighteen-foot ceilings do nothing more than agitate the muggy air. Intermittently, the kitchen doors swing open and one of the crew deposits another platter of country ham, another pan of corn pudding, another skillet of fried chicken on the buffet line.

After the queue dies down, just when I spy another skillet emerging from the kitchen, I head for the buffet and load a plate with drumsticks and thighs and corn pudding. To my surprise, though I'm pretty sure I got my chicken soon after it emerged from the fryer, the crust on my thigh is firm but soft and faintly, just faintly, sweet. I was expecting a brittle crust that cleaved and crumbled with each bite.

Many months later, after talking this over with fellow fried chicken aficionados, I will call upon a number of theories about what advantage the onions offer. Perhaps the sugars in the onions impart a subtle sweetness. Maybe the water released by the onions ensures moistness. But for now, I am blissfully uninformed, munching a thigh enrobed in a soft and sweet mantle.

the next morning, I breakfast on fried flounder and spoonbread, before working up the nerve to ask Dot what she imagines will happen when she and Lucille retire. She does not flinch. "I imagine that when we step down," she says, "they'll stow away those skillets and put in a row of deep fryers."

Debra Donahue, the hotel's marketing manager, is listening to our conversation. She does not argue the point. Instead, she offers a press-kit-ready solution. "If we retire those skillets when Dot and Lucille go," she says, "then what we'll do is mount them on the wall, crossing the handles like a coat of arms." Warming to her idea, she waxes on, "That's it, those skillets, along with Dot and Lucille's names—and their mother's name too—we can mount them on the wall just above the entrance to the Magnolia Room."

It seems a fitting tribute. Sure, it has never been about the skillets, and Debra knows this. Dot and Lucille know this. I know this. We all know that the tradition embodied by those oversized skillets, the lives manifest in their ebony sheen, is best understood in terms of toil, in terms of decades of fourteen-hour days spent on their feet, at the stove. A skillet cannot encapsulate their lives. And much as I would like to think otherwise, neither can this book.

There are many pitfalls to appreciating the likes of Dot and Lucille. Far too many times over the course of my research, I heard well-meaning folk consign a woman's mastery of kitchen craft to some sort of supernatural phenomenon wherein the acquired skill of African American cooks was deemed beyond our reckoning and thus deigned an "expression of soul." That's too pat, too limiting, too freighted with the possibility of denying the richness of experience of the human beings whose hands were ever on the skillet.

I think of Dot Burton and Lucille Thompson as archetypes, in league with cooks of yore, sisters black and white, whose stories I came to know while wandering about America. Among the deities are women like Helen Martin of the Brookville Hotel in Brookville, Kansas; Hattie Bair of the Iron Springs Sanitarium in Steilacoom, Washington; Myrtie Mae Barrett of Myrtie Mae's Homestyle Chicken Dinners in Eureka Springs, Arkansas; and Hattie Moseley of Hattie's Chicken Shack in Saratoga Springs, New York. Their lives, and the loss catalogued upon their deaths, give heft to Calvin Trillin's observation, "A superior fried-chicken restaurant is often the institutional extension of a single chicken-obsessed woman[;] like a good secondhand bookshop or a bad South American dictatorship, it is not easily passed down intact."

Onion-Fried Shore Chicken

CAPE MAY, NEW JERSEY

Onions are all-important to this recipe. They impart sweetness. Or maybe they boost moisture. No matter, the result is a soft crust that tastes like a fusion of chicken skin and baking powder biscuit. While the ladies at the Chalfonte cook their

(*continued*)

onions until they are blackened, I rely upon a more onerous technique that offers the bonus of chicken-perfumed onion rings.

- 1 chicken, cut into 8 pieces if less than 3 pounds, 10 pieces if more than 3 pounds
- 2 tablespoons salt
- 2 tablespoons lemon pepper (the kind without salt)
- 1 cup self-rising flour
- Peanut oil
- 2 medium onions, peeled and sliced into ¾-inch-thick rings
- Salt and black pepper for sprinkling

Season chicken with 1 tablespoon salt and 1 tablespoon lemon pepper. Mix flour, remaining salt, and remaining lemon pepper in a heavy paper or plastic bag. Add two pieces of chicken at a time, shake to coat thoroughly, and shake again upon removal to loosen excess flour. (Do not discard bag with flour.)

Remove floured chicken to a wax-paper- or parchment-lined pan. Let rest for 10 minutes. Pour oil into a skillet at a depth of 1½ inches. When oil reaches 350°, place half the onion rings in the skillet. After 3 or 4 minutes, when the hiss from the water in the onions quiets, remove the onions and discard. Place remaining onion rings in a bowl of cold water and set aside.

Slide dark meat into oil, skin-side down, followed by white meat. Keep oil between 300° and 325° and cook chicken pieces for 12 minutes per side, or until an internal thermometer registers 170° for dark meat, 160° for white. Drain chicken on a wire rack, blotting with paper towels if necessary. Keep oil in skillet. Remove remaining onion rings from water and toss in the flour-filled bag, shaking to coat thoroughly. Fry onion rings in the same oil until brown, sprinkle with salt and pepper, and toss atop chicken. *Serves 4.*

Stand Facing the Stove

the stories of strong women make up the backbone of the American fried chicken story. For women like Dot Burton and Lucille Thompson—as well as Smilka Toplasky, whose story follows—the impulse to stand facing the stove and cook is a matter of livelihood.

But for others, like Ruby Pearl Dowda of Trafford, Alabama, it was a matter of conscience. According to her granddaughter, she was a farmwoman of mixed race who passed for white. To earn a few extra dollars, she raised chickens and tended a truck garden. The men in her family worked the coalmines of northern Alabama and liked to tell people that they were on the wrong side of the Edmund Pettus Bridge— and the issue—when Dr. King and his followers marched to demand voting rights in 1965.

Ruby Pearl Dowda did not march at Selma. She did not lock arms with fellow protesters and sing "We Shall Overcome." But when she saw news reports of trouble down in Birmingham, she gathered eggs from her chicken house, pulled a few hens from the flock, and fried batches of chicken, baked pans of cornbread.

When her men were down in the mines, she took the train into Birmingham and, as the movement flared around her, walked the streets, handing out box lunches tied with twine. "She gave them to every black child who looked hungry," recalls her granddaughter, "to every white child who needed to eat."

THREE

Pahovana Piletina,
That's Fried
Chicken to You

It's a little past noon on Sunday in the burg of Barberton, in north-central Ohio. Church just let out. Traffic on Wooster Street, the main drag, is bumper to bumper, Ford to Chevy. At a wood-paneled corner restaurant known as White House Chicken, a middle-aged woman named Darlene holds forth at a corner table.

"I'll tell you one thing," she says, shaking her finger alternately at her mother, her husband, me. In her other hand is a chicken breast. "The people at Village Inn fry too dark. The coleslaw at Belgrade Gardens is too watery. I don't like the fries at Hopocan Gardens. This is my place. . . . I've been eating chicken at White House for more than forty years, been coming here after church since I was a baby, and I'm telling you that this is what Barberton chicken is supposed to taste like."

Working-class Barberton has been heralded at various times as home of America's largest sewer tile kiln and the match-manufacturing capital of the world. But allegiances are now sworn and epithets hurled in the name of whose bird is freshest, whose crust is crispest. Here fried chicken hearkens back to Serbia, where Smilka Topalsky, the widely acknowledged progenitor of the Barberton chicken phenomenon, was born just north of Belgrade. I came here, hard on the heels of my time in New Jersey, in search of exemplary fried chicken and tales of immigrant life.

Smilka and her husband Milos were accidental restauranteurs. Saddled with debt during the Great Depression, the second-generation Ohioans ceded the family dairy farm on the outskirts of town to the tax collector. But in a typical immigrant bootstrap story, Smilka cooked the family back to solvency by way of bread-crumb-coated fried chicken, vinegary coleslaw, a kind of tomato-rice slurry known as hot sauce, and lard-fried potatoes, served first in the family home and later, around 1933, in the family restaurant, Belgrade Gardens. Topalsky lore holds that these dishes were exacting replications of what Smilka and Milos knew in the Old Country as something like *pahovana piletina, kupus salata, djuvece,* and *pomfrit,* respectively.

Some natives carp that the dishes were not as true to Old World form as the Topalskys and their boosters would have you believe. And to a certain extent, they have a point, for chicken paprikash might have been a more likely crossover contender than fried chicken, and Belgrade Gardens' distinctive hot sauce recalls nothing so much as a spicy riff on TV-dinner-style Spanish rice. But the story of American fried chicken is a tale of assimilation and adaptation. Bread-crumb-coated meat cutlets and poultry parts are staples of many European traditions, from the cookery of Milan to that of Vienna. Such takes on the fried chicken theme become distinctly American as one generation begets the next, as crumbs made with Old World breads are supplanted by pouches sold by Pepperidge Farm.

Over time, the foods that emerged from Smilka Topalsky's kitchen came to be considered core elements of the Barberton chicken story—embraced by all manner of recently immigrated Croats and Hungarians and Slovaks as not so much Serbian, but American. Soon, German and Irish immigrants were sitting alongside Croats and Hungarians and Slovaks. Their points of origin were myriad. Their love of fried chicken brought them to the same table. And in a curious way, fried chicken proved a substantive and symbolic part of their rebirth as polyglot Americans.

Imitators emerged quickly. Another family of Serbs, the

Milichs—who had worked the kitchen and floor at Belgrade Gardens—opened Hopocan Gardens on Hopocan Road in 1946, then served virtually the same chicken, sauce, coleslaw, and potatoes. Like the Toplaskys, they were recently immigrated Serbs. A third Serb, Mary Marinkovich, opened White House Chicken in 1950, and was soon followed by—among other pretenders to the throne—Orchard Inn, Western Star, Terrace Gardens, and The Flagpole.

Today, four of Barberton's old-line chicken dinner restaurants survive: Belgrade Gardens, Hopocan Gardens, Village Inn, and White House Chicken. With the possible exception of Belgrade Gardens, all are best appreciated as linoleum-and-leatherette warhorses, glorified cafeterias that are long on value but short on decor. Perhaps as a consequence, the chicken dinner houses of Barberton do not garner the respect they deserve. In a way it's their own fault, for these restauranteurs have been in the business so long that they are blind to all: their eyeglasses are streaked with lard, their dining-room windows smudged with flour.

One retired chicken man tells me that, a couple years back, Mayor Randy Hart of Barberton suggested that the local reputation for fried fowl was a "stigma" that the community should shed. Barberton was once a workingman's town, but the match factory and the sewer tile kiln and the rubber plant and the boiler factory have all closed. It's now a town scratching about for an identity, a town where the fans of opposing basketball teams mock the Barberton High boys by wearing chicken buckets on their heads. Sadly, it's now a town where such pranks hurt—not because the city's fried chicken heritage hints at some shared underlying foible of Barberton folk—but because the city lacks the vision and mettle to celebrate what distinguishes this burg from thousands of others in Middle America.

That realization gets me down. But it also gets me eating. As a gesture of solidarity, I pledge that, for the remainder of my visit, I will eat not two but three meals a day of Barberton chicken. I even deign to eat at one of the newfangled franchises.

And what do I divine? Halfway through my bacchanal, I decide—just as I did at the Chalfonte—that all Barberton chicken tastes absurdly simple, almost ascetic. When I ask the man or woman on the street why Barberton chicken tastes so good, I hear no talk of secret spice mixes, no discussion of proprietary marinades or breading mixes. And I find comfort in that.

I get similar non-responses from the restauranteurs. Each one I meet, from Sophia Papich, daughter of the Topalskys, to Dale Milich, proprietor of the Village Inn, admits that since most every proprietor is related by blood or marriage or employment history, the chicken recipes and techniques vary little from house to house.

About technique, I'm told: First you roll the chicken in

salted flour. Then you dip it in egg wash. Then you roll it in bread crumbs. Finally you drop it in roiling lard, where it cooks until done.

When we talk philosophy, each restauranteur sketches out the same three tenets: True Barberton chicken is fresh, never frozen. (Most birds are raised by downstate Amish farmers and were pecking about the barnyard a couple of days previous.) True Barberton chicken is seasoned with nothing but a modicum of salt. True Barberton chicken must be cooked in lard, for a great crust requires liquid swine.

And it is to this last tenet that I cleave. Among a certain circle of chicken house connoisseurs, arguments ensue over whose hot sauce is the liveliest, whose coleslaw is the sweetest, whose fries are the crispest, or whose bird is the freshest. But for me, it proves to be all about the crust. And I believe the crust is all about the lard. When prepared in the traditional manner, Barberton chicken emerges from its porcine baptism sheathed in a crisp but slightly chewy coating that even an upstart like me can come to appreciate as the best part of the meal.

Toward that end, on my last day in town, a regular at Belgrade Gardens takes me aside and lets me in on a little secret. He tells me that he loves fried chicken backs—which the restaurant markets as chicken ribs. Though they yield little meat, they offer a wealth of crust to be chomped from the bone. When I look skeptical, my new friend offers a rib, and I am soon gnawing away.

late that same afternoon, on my way to the airport, I place a call to Mayor Hart. I'm thinking that he may not have tried the backs from Belgrade Gardens and that I may be able to help him see the error of his ways. But, according to his secretary, Mayor Hart has no time for me. When pressed, she refuses to posit an opinion about whether His Honor has ever even had the pleasure of gnawing a chicken back.

Serbian-American Fried Chicken

BARBERTON, OHIO

This is simple fried chicken, but it's not simplistic—straight-forward flavors sometimes pack more punch, more appeal, than complex ones. This crust is a thing of beauty, thick and crisp and heady with the slightly porcine flavor that comes from a baptism in roiling lard.

- 1 chicken, cut into 8 pieces if less than 3 pounds, 10 pieces if more than 3 pounds

(*continued*)

- 1 cup all-purpose flour
- 5 teaspoons salt
- 5 teaspoons pepper
- 1 cup unseasoned, untoasted bread crumbs
- 2 eggs, beaten
- Lard, or shortening into which you mix
about 3 tablespoons bacon grease

Combine flour, 2 teaspoons salt, and 2 teaspoons pepper in a large bowl. Combine bread crumbs and 2 teaspoons salt, and 2 teaspoons pepper in another large bowl. Roll chicken pieces in flour mixture and shake off excess. Dip pieces, one by one, in beaten eggs. Roll in bread crumbs, taking care to press crumbs into chicken. Gently shake off excess.

Melt lard or shortening to a depth of at least 3 inches in a heavy, deep kettle. Heat to 300°. Fry chicken pieces for 15 minutes, or until an internal thermometer registers 170° for dark meat, 160° for white meat. Drain on a wire rack, and sprinkle lightly with remaining salt and pepper. *Serves 4.*

Deep-Fried Fowlosophy

In preparation for my visit to Barberton, I turned to the work of anthropologist Sidney Mintz. He argues that to have a cuisine, a locale must boast an informed class of eater, able to proclaim the virtues of a particular dish. Of equal importance, eaters who can tell a true rendition of a dish from an imposter must be willing to fend off challenges to the canon. They must be able to, in the case of Barberton chicken, spot the lone KFC drumstick in a bucket of the good stuff from Belgrade Gardens.

By Mintz's definition, Barberton lays claim to a cuisine. And so does my next destination, Chicago. On the Southside, you're likely to spy a chicken joint on every fifth block. Typical is Eat N Run, the interior of which is painted to resemble a red-and-white-striped circus tent. Omnipresent is Harold's Chicken Shack, a local chain with more than thirty locations. The sign at 83rd boasts that Harold's serves "the chicken that keeps you licking."

Eat N Run and Harold's serve the prevailing Chicago style: deep-fried chicken resting atop a couple slices of white bread and a thatch of fries, the whole affair drenched in a torrent of ketchup-sweet hot sauce, and passed to walkup customers through carousels set in Plexiglas. But I've learned to love an Italianate variant, dished by Chef Luciano. His story follows.

FOUR

Talking Trash and Chicken with the King of the Mutts

C hef Luciano of Gourmet Fried Chicken in Chicago does not suffer fools gladly. Unfortunately, he pegs me for an insufferable fool when, after picking his name out of the yellow pages, I call to ask, "Just what does it mean to serve 'gourmet fried chicken'?"

After harrumphing his contempt, Luciano bellows, "Who in the hell do you think you are, asking a question like that? You don't know what gourmet means? It means that I marinate my chicken in garlic and lemon juice for at least a day. It means that I use fresh chicken. Never frozen. It means that I cook fried chicken like a fine Italian restaurant would!"

When I ask, among other things, whether he uses fresh or powdered garlic for the marinade, Luciano lets fly a second fusillade of invective: "Garlic powder? Garlic powder? That's bullshit! I use fresh garlic, more garlic than any other restaurant in Chicago." And then he repeats his original query, "Who in the hell do you think you are?"

Before I can stammer an answer, Luciano slams down the phone. With the dial tone still ringing in my ear, I begin plotting a visit to his lair. But first, in the interest of better understanding how one would fry chicken in the manner of an Italian gourmet, I do some research. Here's what I learn:

Between 1820 and 1920 more than four million Italians immigrated to America, with most arriving between 1880 and 1920. While it was typical for recently arrived immigrants to settle in enclaves staked out by their countrymen, not every Italian flocked to New York's Greenwich Village or San Francisco's North Beach. Italian men also lit out for the docks of New Orleans, for the coal mining districts of upland Kentucky, for the stockyards of Missouri, Ohio, Iowa, and Illinois. Each destination promised jobs. In exchange for a life of hefting cotton bales or digging coal or gutting swine, immigrants earned their progeny a shot at assimilation, a chance at becoming American.

Typically, when an enclave reached critical mass, one immigrant—perhaps he had been a pasta maker in Naples, maybe

he had cured salami in Genoa—would, frustrated by the short-
age of Italian foodstuffs, open a corner market to serve his
countrymen. Another immigrant, oftentimes a widow in need
of funds, might open her home to boarders. And by these simple acts of commerce, the red-and-white-checked-tablecloth
Italian restaurants of Middle America were born, as corner
markets added plate lunches built around the goods for sale
on their shelves, as boardinghouse *nonne* strove to serve dishes
that Italians (not to mention all manner of other newly arrived
immigrants) might deem palatable.

In the Midwest, where chicken was a farmhouse specialty,
and a bird might easily be penned out back until the time
came to wring its neck, fried chicken became a fixture of
Italian-run roadhouses. It assumed the status of culinary lingua
franca, becoming a dish that bespoke the chicken-in-every-
skillet bounty of America. Granted, fried chicken might have
been served back home. (The recipe at the end of this chapter is from Cesare Casella, a native of Tuscany, who proclaims
a long and proud Tuscan heritage for fried chicken.) But
back home in Italy, fried chicken was not considered iconic.

The fried chicken served in these roadhouses became
iconic—and a shade less Italian—by means of the American
entrepreneurial instinct to codify and then commodify. By
serving Romano-crusted fried chicken alongside spaghetti
with red sauce, joints like Romine's of St. Louis, Gino's of Des
Moines, and, in later years, Maniaci's Café Siciliano of Mil-
waukee acknowledged their ethnic identity while trumpeting
their emergent Americanness.

Chicago, the big-shouldered citadel of opportunity for the working class, was a magnet for Italian immigrants. Some of their old-line restaurants endure to this day. But along the way, more interesting developments came to the fore. That's where my tempestuous friend Luciano comes in, for, though his claim to Italian lineage turns out to be tentative at best, he cooks some of the best Italian-style fried chicken in the land.

Chef Luciano's four-storefront complex is twenty-odd blocks south of the Loop on Cermak Road, at the heart of a neighborhood dominated by midrise housing projects and fast-food restaurants. There are two entrances to his business. On the corner is Gourmet Fried Chicken. Deeper into the block is another take-away stand, Chef Luciano's. Plateglass windows front both, and from those windows glare neon signs. Just inside the vestibule at Chef Luciano's, I spy a placard that advertises, "We do not fry any food in this kitchen." I choose the other entrance.

Don Luciano lords over all. While awaiting my audience, I peruse the menus for both businesses. The Chef Luciano side is comparatively luxe. Celebrity glossies and signed testimonials blanket the walls. Meteorologists, anchormen, political functionaries, and super-chef Charlie Trotter all pledge their love of Luciano. Here he dishes up turkey masala pizza, collard greens sautéed with garlic, chicken piri piri, and jumbo scallops napped in Alfredo sauce. Thirty paces west—under the same roof and in a setting that, owing to its cleanliness and stark white paint, can only be described as institutional—the cooks at Gourmet Fried Chicken dish catfish fillets, chicken wings and legs and breasts, and tubs of red beans and basmati rice.

In due time, Luciano emerges from a dining cubbyhole secreted in the bowels of the restaurant where, behind a false mirror, he watches the comings and goings of guests, oftentimes quaffing a balloon of Chianti or a stem of Champagne. I somehow expected to be greeted by a wizened veteran of the restaurant business, one of those nervous men whose diet seems to be restricted to black coffee and cigarette ash. But Luciano is an ox, a gray-haired bruiser with a birthmark that casts a pall over one side of his face, as if he were forever standing astride a shadow.

I ask about the contradictory messages communicated by his enterprises. I expect another tirade. But Luciano has softened. Maybe it is the wine. Maybe it is my praise of his fried chicken, which, while cooling my heels, I ate with great relish. I was not able to isolate anything specifically gourmet about it, but I can tell you that from first bite to last I tasted garlic, and an herb that might well have been thyme added a contrapuntal mustiness, and the bite of lemon cut through what little grease still clung to the crust. The bird that his employees serve rather unceremoniously by way of bulletproof Plexiglas carousels recalls—though it does not quite equal—the transcendent *pollo fritto* showcased at Beppe, Cesare Casella's temple of Tuscan cuisine in Manhattan.

oon enough, Luciano invites me into his office and takes me into his confidence. Turns out that, though he looks like he might hail from the southern reach of the Boot, he does not boast a single drop of Italian blood. Luciano was born Dave Gupta in New Delhi, India, and immigrated to the United States in 1964 at the age of twenty-four. By dint of sheer will, he landed a job with Moët & Chandon, the white-shoe firm that makes and markets Champagne. At first, Luciano thought he had found his life's work. He reveled in the rich food, the luxe wine.

But while traveling a fourteen-state Midwestern territory he, like legions of salesmen before him, had a bit too much time to think. One day, an isolated observation lodged in his craw: "I saw KFC advertising, 'We do chicken right!' and I thought, 'Now what in the hell does that mean?'" As Luciano's face flushes with blood, he seizes me by the shoulders. "What they do tastes like crap to me," he shouts. "Half of America thinks that's what it tastes like when you do chicken right. That's bullshit! Bullshit, bullshit, bullshit!"

When he calms, Luciano turns reflective. "America is a nation of mutts, of strays," he tells me. "I'm one of them. I'm a mutt who got his start in the restaurant business cooking like I imagined a great Italian chef would. Now people know me for this fried chicken. I tell them, 'Stay off this stuff,' I say, 'Never eat it more than once a week,' I tell them, 'It'll kill you,' but they keep coming, keep eating fried chicken when

I'm trying to convince them to go next door, to try some rapini, taste some eggplant. But what can you do? This is America. We have free will. At least my fried chicken is worth the investment in cholesterol."

I'm beginning to like this guy. What's more, I know that I like his chicken. I have come to appreciate his rant for what it is: pride in craft, pride in tradition. Never mind that the tradition is not his own. After we shake hands, and he withdraws to the Chef Luciano side of the business, I double back for a two-piece drumstick snack. Perhaps he wouldn't approve, but I just can't help myself.

Italian-American Fried Chicken

TUSCANY BY WAY OF CHICAGO AND MANHATTAN

Italian fried chicken is no faddish faux-fusion dish. While researching this book I came across a recipe for Fried Chicken Italienne from the White House Cookbook *of 1887: "Make common batter; mix into it a cupful of chopped tomatoes, one onion chopped, some minced parsley, salt and pep-*

(*continued*)

*per. Cut up young, tender chickens, dry them well, and dip
each piece into the batter; then fry brown in plenty of butter, in
a thick bottom frying pan. Serve with tomato sauce." Better is
this Tuscan fried chicken courtesy of Cesare Casella, chef and
proprietor of Beppe in Manhattan. Think of it as an homage
to Chef Luciano of Gourmet Fried Chicken in Chicago (who
laughed when I asked if he would share his own recipe).*

- 3-to-4-pound chicken, cut into 10 pieces and trimmed of extra fat
- Juice of 2 lemons
- Peanut oil
- 2 cups all-purpose flour
- Salt and pepper to taste
- 2 eggs, beaten lightly and seasoned with salt and pepper
- 2 sprigs fresh thyme
- 2 sprigs fresh rosemary
- 4 cloves garlic
- 1 lemon, cut into wedges

Squeeze lemon juice over the chicken and rub it into the flesh. Cover the chicken with plastic wrap and refrigerate overnight.

Remove from the refrigerator an hour before cooking so that the chicken reaches room temperature.

Pour the oil into a large frying pan until it is one-third full. Heat the oil to 350°. It should not smoke. Mix the flour with some salt and pepper. Dredge the chicken pieces in the flour, then dip them into the beaten eggs. Add the chicken to the pan. Do not over-crowd the pan; there should be plenty of room between pieces. Let the oil drop to a simmer of about 325°. Cook for 15 minutes, or until an internal thermometer registers 170° for dark meat, 160° for white.

During the last 2 minutes before removing the chicken from pan, turn up the heat to 375° to crisp. Then add the herbs and garlic for about a minute. Remove the chicken and herbs from the oil and drain on paper towels. Sprinkle more salt and pepper to taste. Squeeze fresh lemon, and serve on a platter topped with the herbs. *Serves 4.*

Chicken and Stars

If Colonel Sanders was once the poster boy for fried chicken, who or what might replace him tomorrow? What symbol or logo can encompass an America where Italian fried chicken as served in Chicago is cooked by a native of India and sold as in African American takeout stands?

The complexity of the question heightens if you ponder Latin fried chicken. In Los Angeles, I investigate the emerging Hispanic fried chicken phenomenon, spending a good bit of time at a fast-food chain based in Guatemala, which features a rootin', tootin', ten-gallon-hat-wearin' chickadee mascot that evokes a conjoining of Big Bird and Marmaduke.

Los Angeles proves the ideal place to consider iconic images: I glimpse forty-foot muffler men balanced atop garages, and blonde figureheads fronting beauty shops. More to the point, in Santa Monica, I spy a lumbering Oldsmobile with a five-foot rooster head and red wattle on the roof and a rococo fiberglass plume trailing from the trunk.

And on the edge of Koreatown, I visit the studio of graphic designer Amy Inouye, savior of Chicken Boy, a twenty-two-foot chicken-with-bucket sculpture that once graced a local fast-food outlet. Though Inouye has room to store only his bust on the premises, to view Chicken Boy against the tag-sale-in-upheaval backdrop of her studio is to know that a post-modern fried chicken icon may be in the making.

FIVE

Viva Pollo Campero

back in the dark ages, before Pollo Campero opened its first U.S. location, flights to Los Angeles from Guatemala City or San Salvador smelled to high heaven. And heaven smelled a lot like fried chicken.

At the time, it was de rigueur among Latin expatriates returning from a visit to Guatemala or El Salvador, Ecuador, or Nicaragua, to leave their clothes behind when packing for an in-bound U.S. flight, and fill their valises, their backpacks, their duffels with Pollo Campero fried chicken. No Pollo Campero? No hugs for the prodigal son, no kisses for the wayward daughter.

By the mid-1990s, the smell of pollo frito proved so over-whelming that the region's primary carrier, TACA airlines, approached Pollo Campero company officials about hermet-ically sealing all chicken boxes intended for international transport. Pollo Campero demurred, but the inquiry spurred the Guatemalan company, in business since 1971, to consider opening stateside locations to serve a burgeoning Hispanic population.

In April of 2002, to great acclaim and a salsa backbeat, Pollo Campero opened its first U.S. outlet in Los Angeles. During opening week the wait exceeded six hours. Satellite trucks idled on the street, fronted by breathless on-the-scene correspondents documenting the traffic jams that ensnarled Olympic Boulevard. Canny entrepreneurs bought chicken by the gross and sold it for two bucks a drumstick to cash-flush devotees who just couldn't wait in line another moment for a taste of home.

Now the wait tracks at about six minutes—from the time I place my order, to the moment I have my tray and am bound for the pico de gallo bar. On this Thursday afternoon, it's just me, a crew of roofers from the Dominican Republic, and a party of birthday celebrants. I try to engage the roofers in conversation about ethnic identity, about fried chicken, about whether fast-food flour tortillas are preferable to fast-food brown-'n'-serve rolls, but my Spanish fails me, and I can't quite get them to understand my intent.

"Do you consider yourself to be a fan of Pollo Campero?" I ask. "Are you happy to be here? Or is this just another fried chicken joint?" One of the men—whose ability to span the Spanish-English language chasm is obviously more well honed than mine—looks at me with the same wary expression I must wear when those clipboard-wielding survey-takers approach me at the mall. I have a little more luck with the adolescent birthday girl and friends who occupy a corner phalanx of orange fiberglass booths. Above them arch yellow and orange balloons, and behind them a plume of flags frames a larger-than-life rendering of the restaurant's Stetson-wearing mascot, El Pollito Campero. (Call it a new world order as imagined by south-of-the-border poultrymen: the banner of Guatemala is at the center, Mexico is at bottom right, and the U.S. is at bottom left.) On the table is box upon box of chicken. When I approach the birthday girl, a woman I assume to be her mother smiles warmly, shushes the kids, and, before I have a chance to speak, leads the throng in a chant. *"¡Pollo Campero es Guatemala!"* they shout. *"¡Pollo Campero es el mejor pollo!"*

t he chicken I sample is coated in a ferrous-brown crust of lacy texture and is, from first bite to last, juicy and crispy and undeniably good. It's also virtually greaseless. But as good as it is, as much as I enjoy the subtle hint of adobo (the Worcestershire sauce of Hispanic cookery), this chicken does not a phenomenon make. And neither do the rice, the beans, or the salsa verde. Ditto the rice-water drink known as horchata, which, even to an uneducated palate like mine, tastes too much of gritty cinnamon to be truly refreshing. But Pollo Campero *is* a phenomenon. And a wildly successful one at that. Since opening its first Los Angeles franchise, the company has, as of my visit, added two more locations in Los Angeles, and one in Houston. By the time you read this, there may be three in Boise, Idaho.

Back home, Pollo Campero is a pop culture icon, and El Pollito Campero, the mascot, commands his own television cartoon series, sharing billing with Super Camp, his scientist alter ego. Stateside, many believe Pollo Campero to be the Great Brown Hope, the company that will tap into a kind of pan-Latino pride in place and tradition, and take on American-style fast food on its own turf.

Though fried chicken has long been a part of the Latin diet, what seems to capture the attention of a new generation of consumers—and investors—is the Latin yen for fried chicken complemented by the American marketing precepts of cheap and consistent and ever-ready delivery. "We are cheeky, eh?" said Rodolfo Jiménez, Pollo Campero's director of international strategic marketing, to a *New York Times* reporter, soon after the first Los Angeles franchise opened. "At the end of the day, we are selling fried chicken, and what is more American than that?"

won't saddle you with statistics, like the fifty-eight percent
increase in our nation's Hispanic population from 1990
to 2000. I won't burden you with the knowledge that, during
the same period, Hispanic buying power rose from just over
five percent to nearly ten percent of U.S. buying power. No,
that would be boring. You know the impact of Hispanic tastes
and pocketbooks each time you walk down the grocery store
aisle and spot cans of nopalitos beside the green beans, bottles of tamarindo amidst the colas.

Over the course of a year spent wandering the country,
I've eaten—in addition to the Italian and Serbian fried
chicken already discussed—Korean fried chicken in Baltimore, Vietnamese fried chicken in San Francisco, Indian
fried chicken in Dallas, and Szechuan fried chicken in Min-
neapolis. More to the point, I've eaten Latin fried chicken at
a Mexican bodega in Atlanta, at a white-tablecloth bôite in
Chicago, and at a Cuban coffeehouse in Miami.

The best Latin fried chicken I tasted was at New Caporal,
a fast-food take-away in New York City where they marinate
chicken in the garlic-and-citrus concoction known as mojo,
deep fry it, and pile it atop an aerie of curlicue fries. (They
even boast a holster-and-six-shooter-wielding mascot that recalls El Pollito.) Problem is, New Caporal, like the rest of
these chicken purveyors, is singular. Each is a fluke, a con-
spiracy of talent and enterprise that somehow produces a
transcendent piece of fried chicken.

Pollo Campero, on the other hand, is no fluke. It is a corporation dedicated to consistency of product, to sameness of taste. In Latin America, where the company has nearly 200 stores, it sells chicken to parents by way of their children, who are, in turn, seduced by the Saturday-morning superheroes El Pollito and Super Camp. In the United States, Pollo Campero sells itself as an answer to KFC, a taste of home that all Latins can afford and that, if Pollo Campero has its way, all Latins will come to claim as their own.

And therein lies their genius, for what Pollo Campero is *truly* selling to émigrés is a sort of pan-national pride: By the very act of eating this Latin product you are remaking your American experience on your own terms. And at a time when the majority of the line workers in the American poultry industry are Hispanic, in a day when salsa and ketchup do battle for primacy alongside tortillas and white bread, the market is theirs to seize.

Latin American Fried Chicken

LOS ANGELES, CALIFORNIA

The smoky whang of adobo is essential here. It's easy to find in most grocery stores. No whining: If I can find chipotles in adobo at the Kroger in my small whitebread Mississippi town, then you can find it where you live. (I buy the small cans of chipotles in adobo, drain the adobo, and save the chipotles for another use.) This dish was inspired by the fried chicken served by the Pollo Campero, born in Guatemala, and soon to be frying in a town near you.

- 6 chicken leg quarters, cut into thighs and drumsticks
- 2 cups cider vinegar
- 6 tablespoons adobo sauce
- 1 tablespoon salt
- 1 tablespoon Mexican oregano
- ½ cup cornflour (You can use fish fry, but if it's seasoned, reduce salt accordingly.)
- ½ cup all-purpose flour
- 2 cups lard, or 2 cups shortening into which you mix about 3 tablespoons bacon grease

(continued)

Pour vinegar and then adobo sauce into a large glass bowl or pan and stir to combine. Place chicken in marinade and refrigerate for at least 12 hours and no more than 18. Mix salt, oregano, cornflour, and flour in a paper bag. Scoop lard or shortening into a large pot, and melt to a depth of at least 3 inches. Heat over medium-high until thermometer registers 325°. Lift chicken pieces one by one from marinade, allowing excess to drip off before tossing in the bag. Again shake off excess before slipping pieces, skin-side down, into oil. Keep temperature at 325° and fry 15 minutes, or until an internal thermometer registers 170° for dark meat, 160° for white meat. Remove white chicken before dark. *Serves 6.*

Mojo-Marinated Fried Chicken

NEW YORK (WITH A TASTE OF MIAMI)

Here's another Latin favorite. Mojo sauce, traditionally prepared with sour oranges (lime juice and an orange are used here), is the marinade of choice for many Cuban dishes. (If you've ever eaten a Cuban sandwich, mojo is the marinade that gives punch to the filling of roast pork.) Though I've eaten this take on fried chicken at ten or twelve different spots, this version owes its style to my recollections of the chicken fried at New Caporal in New York, and a panel-truck commissary parked a few blocks off Calle Ocho in Miami.

- 1 chicken, cut into 8 pieces if less than 3 pounds, 10 pieces if more than 3 pounds
- 3 cloves garlic, chopped fine
- 2 bay leaves
- 2 cups lime juice, fresh squeezed
- 1 onion, sliced thin
- 1 teaspoon cumin, ground
- ½ cup all-purpose flour
- Peanut oil

(*continued*)

- ■ 1 clove garlic, peeled
- ■ 1 orange, unpeeled and cut into 10 slices

Combine chopped garlic, bay leaves, lime juice, onion, and cumin in a large bowl. Place chicken in the same bowl, submerge in marinade, cover with plastic wrap, and place in refrigerator for at least 8 hours and as many as 12. Remove from marinade and drain on a wire rack.

Place flour in a paper bag and toss chicken in, a couple of pieces at a time. Pull chicken from the bag, shaking each piece very well so the barest dusting covers. Pour oil into a heavy and high-sided chicken-fryer or Dutch oven to a depth of at least 3 inches. Add garlic clove.

Heat oil over medium-high to a temperature of 325° (leaving garlic in until it turns dark brown), and fry chicken for 15 minutes, or until an internal thermometer registers 170° for dark meat, 160° for white meat. Squeeze a slice of orange over each piece and place slice atop. *Serves 4.*

Hunting and Pecking for
Smoked and Fried

have you ever eaten chicken that was barbecued, battered, and fried? Since I first tasted pork ribs prepared that way at Little Dooey's in Columbus, Mississippi, I've been searching for a chicken analogue.

At Stevie's on the Strip in Los Angeles, they once smoked their birds before frying them, but quit because, in the words of the cashier, "liquid smoke got too expensive." I plotted a trek to Simply Southern in Las Vegas, reputedly famous for "hickory fried chicken." But when I phoned, the number had been disconnected. I made a return trip to AQ Chicken in Springdale, Arkansas, where I had once liked their "chicken over the coals." AQ works the dish backward, frying and then chargrilling. This time around, my thigh tasted more acrid than smoky. I have yet to make it to Keaton's in Cleveland, North Carolina, but I'm in no hurry, because I understand that, instead of smoking and then frying, they do nothing more than fry chickens and then dunk them in barbecue sauce.

I'm a bit dispirited, yet I continue to query friends and colleagues. Most, when I pledge my unrequited love of smoked and then fried chicken, look at me like I'm crazy. Come to think of it, they look at me the same way when I pledge my requited love of fried chicken and waffles.

SIX

Of Wattles and Waffles

i came upon many an odd dish while eating my way toward a theory of American fried chicken. But none seemed to stymie family and friends more than fried chicken and waffles. At first blush, the dish defies logic: savory fried chicken served *atop*, or sometimes *alongside*, battercake waffles drenched in butter and syrup.

If this combination is new to you, if it seems novel, you are not alone. I did not experience my first dish of chicken and waffles until 1998, at Gladys Knight and Ron Winans's Chicken and Waffles on Peachtree Street in Atlanta, Georgia. There I ate the "Midnight Train," four jumbo wings and a waffle.

Even today, many restaurants consider chicken and waffles to be so novel that they append to their menu instructions on how to consume it. One Ohio spot details an eleven-step process that dictates, among other intricacies, sprinkling hot sauce on the chicken, sluicing syrup on the waffle, and spearing a bit of each with your fork.

Chicken and waffles has infiltrated all manner of pop culture. Remember the Quentin Tarantino movie *Jackie Brown,* wherein Samuel Jackson's character, Ordell, baits one of his flunkies with the promise of dinner at Roscoe's Chicken and Waffles? Or the scene in *Swingers* where Mike and Trent and the boys caravan to Roscoe's for a late-night feed? Or the faux commercial for Roscoe's in the John Cusack satire *Tapeheads*?

Well, neither do I, but legions of hipsters remember these scenes. What's more, those hipsters—and their boho parents before them—have been wolfing down chicken and waffles for decades, maybe even a couple of centuries. Most pop culture references I chronicle above point to Roscoe's Chicken and Waffles of Hollywood (established circa 1975) as ground zero for the phenomenon. Though I have no hard evidence to back my supposition, I believe that the combination may have been a fixture of the American table since the early years of our republic when Thomas Jefferson returned from France with a goose-handled waffle iron, and, by championing the treat, ushered in a kind of waffle craze.

———

i n an attempt to establish an earlier debut, I have a bit
of corroboration. Sallie Creuzot of Frenchy's Chicken in
Houston told me that she grew up in Virginia, in the years
leading up to World War II, eating a Sunday breakfast of fried
chicken and waffles. Edna Lewis, the grande doyenne of
African American cooks, writes in her first book that fried
chicken was a popular breakfast dish of her youth. In *The
United States Regional Cookbook,* published in 1939, the Southern section features a recipe for "Kentucky Fried Chicken"
that is steamed until tender, batter-fried, and served with
griddlecakes, grits, or—you guessed it—waffles.

And then there are the near misses: In *Dishes & Beverages of
the Old South,* published in 1913, Martha McCullough-Williams
provides a recipe for waffles and advises that while syrup is appropriate, "it is profane to drench them with it—strong clear
coffee, and broiled chicken are the proper accompaniments
at breakfast." And the unconfirmed rumors, like the one I
heard about an edition of Emily Post's etiquette guide that
suggests bachelors use Saturday afternoon picnic leftovers or
a bucket of takeout to accessorize a Sunday waffle brunch.

Further afield are the Pennsylvania Dutch. In *Sauerkraut
Yankees,* the esteemed historian William Woys Weaver argues
that waffles were oftentimes the preferred ballasts for chicken
dishes. While the Pennsylvania Dutch were more likely to eat
creamed chicken atop their waffles, Will's work does nothing
but cement my theory that the pairing of fried chicken and

waffles is elemental. Such thinking puts the dish in league with tearoom delicacies like creamed chicken on toast points and not too far removed from a farmwoman's Sunday dinner of fried spring chicken with hoecakes or biscuits, served with all manner of jams and preserves, maybe even a jug of cane syrup.

Jeffrey Steingarten, the erudite eater and author, exposed one of the more delicious threads of investigation. Herb, the owner of the five-site Roscoe's chain, told Jeffrey that the key to understanding the sweet side of the combo lay in examining the historical affinity of biscuits and molasses. I found this insight intriguing, but, when I traveled to Los Angeles, could not gain access for further questioning. After my third call for an interview, Herb's secretary said, "He's a very busy man." With apparent befuddlement over my passion and genuine pity for my plight, she added, "You'll have more luck getting an interview with the President."

I can't blame Herb. I must appear a madman, squandering my days, trying to find the alpha fried chicken and waffles cook. It's a task with as many pitfalls as determining out of what tradition, from what peoples, came fried chicken itself.

We do know this: the tradition of cooking in deep oil has probable West African antecedents. Figure in that much early American kitchen work was thrust upon enslaved Africans. Beyond that, tracing the origins of fried chicken is a frustrating exercise. Perhaps it will suffice to observe that, in the eighteenth century—while cooking for (and sometimes under the direction of) white slaveholders—women of African descent honed a dish we now know as fried chicken. And then just leave it at that.

When it comes to fried chicken and waffles, however, clarity evades me. Part of the problem is that, the more I research, the more I uncover competing views: Hanibal Tabu, a Los Angeles restaurant reviewer, argues that chicken and waffles is the "traditional breakfast of Southern black folk who wouldn't eat pork." While that's a bit dubious, Robb Walsh, dining critic for the *Houston Press*, suggests cannabis at the root of the phenomenon. "Like pretzels and chocolate ice cream," he writes, it's a "come-home-stoned, stand-in-front-of-the-refrigerator kind of concoction."

The Convention Visitors Bureau of Oakland, California (the city is home to at least two purveyors), refers to chicken and waffles as a Louisiana dish, their logic being, one assumes, that odd edibles must come from the land of paunce and turducken. Across the bay, the *San Francisco Chronicle* claims that Roscoe's owes its culinary shtick to a spot called Will's Chicken and Waffles in Harlem. Speaking of Harlem, Carl Redding, proprietor of Amy Ruth's, claims that his grandmother, Amy Ruth Bass of Gordon, Alabama, taught him to cook and appreciate chicken and waffles.

Most Harlem origin stories point to the now defunct Wells Supper Club, opened in 1938 by Joseph Wells, an icon of early-to-mid-twentieth-century pop culture. Nat King Cole held his wedding reception at Wells. Sammy Davis, Jr., and the Rat Pack slouched and drank there. Sidney Poitier owned a rib joint on the same block. Count Basie had a club next door. And if the stories I am told are to be believed, everyone seems to have subsisted on a diet of chicken and waffles, the signature dish of Wells Supper Club.

But Wells Supper Club was, more than likely, just the Roscoe's of another time, a place that popularized a dish already ensconced in the folk repertoire. Bunny Berigan, a hard-living trumpet player who died of cirrhosis at the age of thirty-three, cut a single, "Chicken and Waffles," for Decca in 1935—three years before locals believe that Joseph Wells even opened his supper club. In other words, Wells—and in later years, Roscoe's—probably had the same impact upon chicken and waffles that Hunt's, merchandiser of the Manwich, had on the Sloppy Joe.

In addition to the aforementioned Amy Ruth's, many modern-day Harlem restaurants still sell chicken and waffles, including Miss Maude's Spoonbread Too, Pan Pan Diner, Sugar Shack Cafe, and Hip Hop Chicken and Waffles. And we're just getting started. Beyond the Hudson River, Sham-Danai's of Baltimore serves chicken and waffles. So does Jones in Philadelphia, a fieldstone-flanked living room posing as a restaurant. In our nation's capital, B. Smith's at Union Station serves chicken and waffles with onion gravy. At the Breakfast Klub in Houston, Marcus Davis and crew spike their waffles with cinnamon. And don't forget the Motown Café in Universal City, Florida, where in addition to "Ain't No Ham and Rye Enough" and "Marvelettes Motown Sampler" (a soulful pu pu platter) they offer "It Takes Two Chicken and Waffles," described on the menu as a "traditional dish."

What restaurant will emerge as the next Wells or Roscoe's? Until recently, my money was on Phil Davis, owner of the restaurant Phil the Fire in Cleveland, Ohio. He's an ardent disciple of the tradition who got hooked on Roscoe's Chicken and Waffles while a student at Stanford University and, once hooked, even journeyed to Harlem to sit at the feet of Joseph Wells's widow, Elizabeth. Until he closed his restaurant in 2004, Phil envisioned dozens of Phil the Fire locations throughout the country and had begun promoting a new product, the Jake Waffle (named for the local baseball stadium, Jacob's Field), for which he sautéed boneless breast strips, then baked them into a waffle and served them with tubs of hot sauce and syrup. Response was positive, and a patent was pending. And then, sadly, Phil the Fire was gone.

Deep-Fried Buttermilk-Bathed Chicken

CLEVELAND, LOS ANGELES,
NEW YORK, AND POINTS BEYOND

I'm usually a dark meat fan, but here breasts are best, for they allow you to more easily slice off a bit of meat, spear a chunk of syrup-drenched waffle, and eat chicken and waffles in the cor-

(*continued*)

rect manner. The Tabasco is also important, for the heat and
the tang play well off the syrup, resulting in a sweet-and-sour
taste reminiscent of Szechuan and Cantonese Chinese cooking.

- 6 chicken breasts, cut in half crossways
- 4 teaspoons salt
- 3 cups buttermilk (or, if you can find only
  cultured buttermilk, 2 cups plain yogurt,
  thinned with 1 cup whole milk)
- 4 tablespoons Tabasco sauce
- 1½ cups all-purpose flour
- 3 teaspoons black pepper
- 3 teaspoons cayenne
- Peanut oil
- 3 slices bacon, chopped

Arrange chicken in one layer in dish or dishes. Sprinkle
with 2 teaspoons salt. Pour buttermilk or thinned yogurt,
spiked with Tabasco, over chicken. Marinate, turning
often, for at least 4 hours and as long as 24. Combine
flour, remaining salt, and pepper and cayenne in a
shallow dish or bowl. Pour oil into a large pot to a depth
of at least 3 inches. Add bacon. Heat over medium-high
until thermometer registers 300°. Remove bacon when
it browns and has rendered all flavor.

Lift chicken pieces one by one from marinade, allowing excess to drip off before coating in seasoned flour. Again shake off excess before slipping pieces, skin-side down, into oil. Keep temperature at 300–325° and fry 12–15 minutes, or until an internal thermometer registers 170° for dark meat, 160° for white meat. Drain on a wire rack and turn your attention to the making of waffles as below. *Serves 6.*

Late-Night (or Early-Morning) Waffles

- 1 cup all-purpose flour
- 1 cup stone-ground cornmeal (yellow or white)
- ½ teaspoon baking soda
- 2 teaspoons baking powder
- 1 teaspoon salt

(continued)

- ▪ 2 eggs, separated into yolks and whites
- ▪ 1¾ cups buttermilk
- ▪ 4 tablespoons melted butter
- ▪ Rendered fat from 3 slices bacon

Combine flour, cornmeal, baking soda, and baking powder. Sift, or, if you're feeling lazy, stir well with a fork. In a separate bowl, beat egg yolks well. Add buttermilk, butter, and bacon fat to yolks and stir. Add the liquid to the dry ingredients and combine with four or five strokes of a whisk. (Do not overwork the batter, for it will toughen.) Beat egg whites until stiff and fold gently into batter. Cook 4–6 minutes according to waffle iron directions, or until steam ceases leaking from beneath the lid.

Serve with cane or maple syrup and a bottle of Louisiana hot sauce (or any of the more viscous brands). *Serves 6.*

Hand in the Honey Pot

t he marriage of salty and sweet isn't newfangled. Nor is it singular. Fried chicken drizzled with honey is the dish of record at Nick's Family Restaurant in Kingsport, Tennessee, where they pressure-fry chicken and set tables with bear-shaped honey dispensers. Al's Chickenette of Hays, Kansas, considers honey pots de rigueur. The Kennon House in Gasburg, Virginia, serves fried chicken with a single packet of honey, but if you ask for three they'll oblige.

Chez Haynes, an American fried chicken outpost in Paris, France, pours honey atop their birds. So does Julep, a tony Southern restaurant in Jackson, Mississippi, where cooks infuse the honey with rosemary. Greenwood's on Green Street in Roswell, an Atlanta suburb, dunks fried chicken in Georgia mountain honey and then pours on pepper vinegar.

During the 1960s, there was even a chain, Yogi Bear's Honey Fried Chicken. James Beard, the dean of American gastronomes, paid homage to their version of the dish in his seminal work, *American Cooking*, but he failed to make note of the chain's modest and oddly affecting slogan—a tip of the hat to Yogi—"Better Than Your Average Chicken."

SEVEN

Cock-A-Doodle Don't

they were halcyon, those days before the first fast-food lawsuit was filed in 2002, before restaurant chains came to represent rapid and, by extension, vapid homogenization of our nation's food supply. Nowadays, nutritionists decry that purveyors of fast-food fried chicken and burgers and fries are nothing more than fat-and-cholesterol-delivery outlets. And plaintiffs' attorneys, who earned their chops battling Big Tobacco, have begun calling fast food's parent companies Big Food.

Driving the byways of America in search of meaning, I tend to discount the fast-food medium as message. But what could be more real, more American? Way back when, fast food was novel, even hip.

The year was 1969. The place was Nashville, Tennessee. Kentucky Fried Chicken, which had gone public with the backing of a local businessman, would, in that one year, earn more than twelve million dollars for its investors. Newspapers were full of stories of secretaries who became overnight tycoons when they cashed in early stock investments. It had been five years since founder Harlan Sanders, who leveraged his roadside motel court and restaurant into a 600-unit chicken chain, sold his stake in the company—not to mention his technique of quick-frying chicken in a pressure-cooker and his secret recipe containing eleven herbs and spices.

He was now five years into a round-the-world promotional tour on behalf of the Kentucky Fried Chicken corporation. In exchange for a generous annual fee, the honorary Kentucky colonel was the white-haired, string-tied, public face of the corporation. A born showman, Sanders was keen on kissing babies, shaking hands, and spreading the gospel according to Kentucky Fried Chicken. At the core of the gospel was the promise of riches. Untold riches. And Nashville was giddy over future prospects.

In 1969, along with a group of investors, Minnie Pearl, the Grand Ole Opry comedian famous for her homespun humor, had secured commitments for a chain of fried chicken houses: 1,400 locations of Minnie Pearl's Fried Chicken.

Interior designers used her trademark hat—the flower-bedecked one that famously trailed a $1.95 price tag—as inspiration for the chain's color palette.

Minnie was not alone in her attempt to ride the wave breached by Harlan Sanders. Eddy Arnold, known to fans as "the Tennessee Plowboy," was selling franchise licenses for Eddy Arnold's Tennessee Fried Chicken. Even Little Jimmie Dickens, who rose to fame singing "Take an Old Cold Tater and Wait," opened a restaurant.

The rapidly escalating number of Nashville-based fried chicken franchises captured the attention of parodists Homer and Jethro. They recorded a lament, "There Ain't a Chicken Safe in Tennessee." Not to be outdone, Billy Edd Wheeler cut "Fried Chicken and a Country Tune." Over a banjo backbeat he sang:

> *They started a bunch of corporations*
> *Everybody got into speculation*
> *Chicken stock was so alarming*
> *Nearly made Dow Jones go back to farmin'* . . .
>
> *Selling fried chicken and a country tune*
> *They go together like a moon in June*
> *Finger-lickin' chicken and a diddle-i-doon*
> *Fried chicken and a country tune.*

Some entrepreneurs looked beyond Nashville's Grand Ole Opry for inspiration. The same businessmen who backed

Minnie Pearl devised a franchise plan built around gospel recording artist Mahalia Jackson. (Benjamin Hooks, Jr., who would go on to become the president of the NAACP, was hired as the front man.) When Aretha Franklin opened a namesake fried chicken chain, James Brown, the Godfather of Soul, answered with the Golden Platter. By the mid-1970s, Chicken George's was in business in Baltimore, pegging its name to the popularity of a character in Alex Haley's epic novel *Roots*. Even Mickey Mantle got in the act, overseeing a country cooking restaurant that advertised, "To get a better piece of chicken, you'd have to be a rooster."

The great majority of these franchises, and many more besides, have come and gone. But none enjoyed such a meteoric rise and fall as Minnie Pearl's Fried Chicken. Investors watched their stock crest and then, in 1970, crash. Problems were of two sorts: The principals had unreasonable expectations of growth and income. And, of even greater importance, they did not know how to fry chicken. Harlan Sanders had spent more than thirty years refining his recipe, traveling the back roads of America in search of restauranteurs who might share his vision. But the principals in Minnie Pearl's were the precursors of today's corporate shysters, churning overvalued assets and siphoning off the cream.

Sanders was known for his bluntness. He once declared that the corporate types at Kentucky Fried Chicken headquarters had bastardized his beloved chicken until it tasted like "nothing more than a fried doughball wrapped around some chicken." Evidently, he chose not to comment on Minnie Pearl's product.

or every crass attempt to cash in, though, there was an entrepreneur determined to pay homage to his or her forebears by building a roadside restaurant and illuminating it with suitable neon candlepower that the whole world might step back to take a gander. I choose to see something uniquely American, something charmingly vainglorious, in one man's willingness to stake fame and fortune upon his mother's special chicken seasoning.

As director of the Southern Foodways Alliance, an organization that studies the traditional food cultures of my native region, I admit that I am a bit biased against the big chains that buy their popsicle chicken by the reefer and their flour by the silo. Yet I can appreciate a fried chicken chain at a liminal stage in its evolution, just after it opens its second or third location and just before the accountant tells the owner, in order to keep food costs in line, "You need to start substituting domestic ginger for the Jamaican stuff now in your spice mix." And while you're at it, "Put away your childish notions of what makes for good marketing. No more dressing up like a drumstick and standing by the curb, clucking to the kids."

There's a certain appeal to a small chain with outsized ambitions, fronted by a man or woman who is just this side of megalomania. In the 1983 movie *Stroker Ace*, a NASCAR champion aligns himself with fried chicken magnate Clyde Torkle. Stroker Ace's contract requires him to wear a chicken suit for commercials and publicity stunts. And soon he's wearing that very chicken suit while driving the banked ovals at more than a hundred miles an hour in a stock car emblazoned with the slogan, "Fastest Chicken in the South."

I think I would have liked Clyde Torkle's fried chicken. I also bet I would have liked Chicken in the Rough, an Oklahoma-based chain that served its chicken "unjointed and without silverware," nestled amidst a "rough" of shoestring potatoes. (The chain's cigar-smoking mascot was a rooster who held a driver in his webbed foot and always seemed to be losing his ball in the grassy rough of a golf course.)

And I admire the entrepreneurial pluck of Norma Young of Searcy, Arkansas. In 1971 she was chosen as a United States Poultry Ambassador and, in the discharge of those duties, toured seven European countries. I have an inkling that, despite the lack of a bone in her 1971 National Chicken Cooking Contest–winning Dipper's Nuggets, I would have liked those too. (The dish was a precursor to the Chicken Mc-Nugget, served with a choice of pineapple, dill, or royalty sauces.) In 1997, at the age of eighty-five, she sold Chicken Twisters, a new recipe concept, to KFC for a tidy sum of money. If Young decided to open a chicken chain, I would be at her door, money in hand.

But all the compelling tales of fried chicken entrepreneurs are not tales of yore. While on the road, I discovered Zeke's Smokehouse in the Los Angeles exurbs, where Mike Rosen mans the fryers. The place feels a little too slick, and the cutesy Labrador mascot looks a little too ready for prime time. But the battered and fried Chicken Littles—the drumstick-

shaped half of the wing, known to the trade as drumettes—
are good enough to merit a return trip.

During that return trip, Rosen owns up to his expansion
plans. He also tells me that, while working at a Hollywood
restaurant, he cadged the batter recipe from an English gent
who was pining for a taste of his native fish and chips. Come
to think of it, the fritterlike puffiness of his Chicken Littles
does call to mind the product of a top-flight Long John Sil-
ver's franchise.

a while back, I searched a database of business names,
hoping that, despite what everyone told me, I might
find a lone Minnie Pearl's Fried Chicken that was still in business. I reasoned that I owed them a tasting and, failing that, I
might locate one of the table tents the company used in the
day, the ones blazoned with the slogan "Howdylicious!" Only
one possibility, Minnie Pearl's Pies in Westwego, Louisiana,
seemed even worth exploring, but the woman who answered
the phone said, "I have nothing to do with *that* Minnie Pearl.
For one thing, she's dead and I'm alive. For another, Minnie
Pearl is my given name—that woman you're talking about,
that wasn't her real name, that name was for the stage. And
plus, I don't fry a thing here."

It seems that the only memory of Minnie Pearl's fried food
reign is kept alive by a smart-aleck restaurateur who batters
and fries pearl onions and calls them—you guessed it—
Minnie Pearls. I had a bit more luck when I tried the same

search for her black analogue, Mahalia Jackson's Fried
Chicken, for which I scored two hits. It seems that octogenarian E.W. Mayo of Nashville has been biding his time since the
1970s, waiting for the chance to revive the chain and take it
nationwide. Though locals tend to prefer his fried pies to her
fried chicken, I would not count Mayo out. "I've got big
plans," he told me recently, "and a mean recipe for fried
chicken. We're on our way, I tell you, on our way."

Honey & Rosemary–Gilded Fried Chicken

JACKSON, MISSISSIPPI

*I did not discover this dish until late in my research. After
traveling clear across the continent in search of fried chicken,
I found this exemplary bird right in my home state at Julep, a
Jackson restaurant run by family friends Patrick and Mary
Kelly. The use of honey reminded me of a similar dish I en-
joyed at Greenwood's on Green Street in Roswell, Georgia.
But while Bill Greenwood cut the honey with a dose of pepper
vinegar, chef Derek Emerson of Julep relies upon the resiny*

bouquet of rosemary. I like both ways. Here's a recipe to get you started.

- 1 chicken, cut into 8 pieces if less than
3 pounds, 10 pieces if more than 3 pounds
- 1 cup all-purpose flour
- 1 tablespoon garlic powder
- 1 tablespoon salt
- 1 tablespoon white pepper
- 1 cup buttermilk
- Peanut oil
- ¾ cup honey
- 1 tablespoon butter
- 1 small sprig rosemary, chopped
- Pepper vinegar (optional)

Mix flour with garlic powder, salt, and pepper. Dip chicken in seasoned flour, then buttermilk, then seasoned flour again. Pour 1½ inches of oil into skillet and heat over medium-high. When the oil reaches 325°, slip the dark meat in, skin-side down, followed by the white meat. Keep the oil between 300° and 325° and cook each side for 5–6 minutes covered and then 5–6 minutes uncovered, for a total of 20–24 minutes, or until an internal thermometer registers 170° for

(*continued*)

dark meat, 160° for white meat. Drain on a wire rack, blotting with paper towels as necessary.

Meanwhile, combine honey, butter, and rosemary in a metal mixing bowl. Place over low to medium burner until butter melts. Stir to combine. Drizzle glaze over chicken, and, if you are so inclined, splash with pepper vinegar like the good folks at Greenwood's. *Serves 4.*

Chain-Gang Chicken

though New Orleans boasts one of the more refined and insular food cultures in the country, the city is not absent chains. All the burger boys have outposts here. But even they must do battle with local multi-units like Lee's Hamburgers and Bud's Broiler.

In most matters, local tastes prevail. Such entrenchment shines through brightest in the matter of fried chicken. Local boy Al Copeland introduced the spicy chicken concept to the world through Popeye's, which he founded in 1971 and which now boasts more than 1,600 locations worldwide.

There have been other contenders. Mama's Tasty Fried Chicken, which sells gizzards on a stick just off St. Charles

Avenue, once had aspirations of expansion. Even Austin Leslie, whom we meet next, once had a franchise plan. But no one truly challenged Popeye's local dominance until December of 2001 when Jane and Scott Wolfe, whom New Orleanians knew as the proprietors of Wagner's Meats (their slogan: "You Can't Beat Wagner's Meat"), opened the first Chicken Box.

The Wolfes deeply undercut Popeye's on price while serving a product that purposefully lacks the spicy punch of cayenne. "Tastes Like Ya Mama's" was one of the company's first slogans. Chicken Box is expanding rapidly, buoyed by an unconventional advertising campaign. A recent Valentine's Day promotion promised free marriages performed with every 1,000-piece order. "We wanted to offer a free divorce," Jane Wolfe told me, "but the lawyers told us that might be tricky."

EIGHT

Austin Leslie,
Creole Comet

he is the oldest cook in the kitchen by a good decade, maybe two. Gray hair mushrooms from beneath his gold-crested captain's hat. A patchwork of broiler scars—the proud tattoos of a life at the stove—blankets the underside of his forearms. By all rights he's too aged, too revered to be working the fryer five nights a week at Jacques-Imo's, New Orleans's most funkadelic restaurant. The first time I saw him perched over a sputtering vat of peanut oil, I was tempted to ask my waitress something like, *Just how did the grand old man of Creole cuisine end up at a renegade restaurant owned by an elfin New York émigré?*

austin Leslie was once the most celebrated Creole-soul cook in New Orleans, and his fried chicken was considered a definitive dish in the native culinary lexicon. For much of the 1970s and '80s, his restaurant, Chez Helene, drew both Garden District swells and Creoles of Color who, emboldened by rave reviews in the press, made their way to North Robertson Street in the Tremé neighborhood for a taste of the city's best back-of-town foods.

Today, though the locus for the pilgrimage has changed, the draw for sojourners remains strong. And so it is that, early in my fried chicken quest, I seek an audience with Leslie. Seated at an oilcloth-clad table at Jacques-Imo's, we sample ruddy drumsticks crowned with his signature confetti of chopped garlic and parsley, and topped with his secret grease-cutting weapon, a slice of dill pickle. As we eat, I learn that Leslie was an unlikely media darling. Born to a mother who worked as a domestic and a father who gambled, he took to the streets at an early age, earning his keep doing odd jobs. "By the time I was around eight or so, I was working for this lady," he says. "She grew different herbs in her yard and I'd sell them for her. I made something like two or three cents off a bunch."

While he was in middle school, Leslie pedaled a bicycle, delivering fried chicken for Portia's Fountain on Rampart Street. "Back then, that was the black Bourbon Street," says

Leslie. "They were always telling me I was too little to work Rampart, but I proved myself. The owner, Bill Turner, he looked after me, he educated me on how restaurants worked. That's where I picked up a lot of what I know about fried chicken, where I learned how to season it right."

After high school came a tour of duty in Korea, a turn in his aunt Helen DeJean Pollock's lunchroom, and a brief stint as a sheet-metal worker. In 1959, Leslie finally hit his stride, when he landed a job as an assistant chef at the restaurant in D. H. Holmes Department Store on Canal Street. "I had grown up walking by there, hearing the dishes clatter and smelling the food," he says. "And then all of a sudden I was working in that big kitchen. I learned how to make oysters Rockefeller and shrimp remoulade."

In 1964, Leslie's aunt Helen moved her lunchroom to new quarters on North Robertson Street, adding an *e* to her name for a touch of class and dubbing the little café Chez Helene. Her nephew followed. "I brought in the dishes I learned at Holmes," recalls Leslie. "It was kind of like integration: a little bit of theirs, a little bit of ours. My aunt already had the greens and yams and jambalaya." When Pollock retired in 1975, Leslie bought her out. In time, all of New Orleans was abuzz with tales of the little neighborhood restaurant where they served tin pie plates of broiled oysters in a velveteen Rockefeller sauce and chipped white platters piled high with the best fried chicken known to man.

At a time when America was awakening to the possibilities of marketing regional cuisine, Leslie was a hot property. By the mid-'80s, rumor had it that he was on the verge of becoming the black Creole analogue to white Cajun Paul Prudhomme. It helped that Leslie—his smiling face framed by a swooping pair of muttonchops, a diamond-encrusted crab pendant around his neck—knew he was selling more than fried chicken. "Yeah, I could talk," he says. "When folks wanted to talk about New Orleans food, I was the man. Difference was, I could cook too, and a lot of those other people couldn't. I could back up my arrogance."

Business partnership offers poured in. Plans were drawn up for a chain of fried chicken restaurants. Upscale branch locations of Chez Helene opened, first in the French Quarter, later in Chicago, Illinois. "Seems like every other day somebody was wanting to talk with me about some kind of great deal," recalls Leslie. "Seems like everybody wanted to use my name to sell this, my face to sell that. I made the mistake of listening."

In March of 1987, Hollywood came calling, in the form of actor Tim Reid, who had previously played the character Venus Flytrap on the show *WKRP in Cincinnati.* Producer Hugh Wilson and he stopped in for dinner, and when they left a few hours later, they were convinced that they had found the restaurant around which they could build a hit television show. The story line was this: Upon the death of his estranged father, Frank Parish, a black professor of Italian Renaissance history in Boston, inherits the family business, a corner bar and restaurant in New Orleans called Chez Louisiane, thus prompting a rediscovery of his own cultural and culinary heritage.

Leslie signed on as a consultant, traveling to California to supervise construction of the kitchen set. He also acted as an informal adviser, coaching the writers and actors on the vagaries of New Orleans diet and dialect. Under Leslie's tutelage, Tony Burton, who played Big Arthur McCormick, the head cook at the fictional Chez Louisiane, and Tim Reid, who played the part of Parish, came to understand mirlitons and muffulettas, Cajuns and Creoles.

Frank's Place debuted in September of 1987. Though it was a critical success, garnering an Emmy award for Wilson and winning a loyal cadre of fans, CBS canceled it exactly a year later. Some network suits cited gritty themes and low ratings, others a budget that made *Frank's Place* the most expensive thirty minutes on television. Wilson himself admitted that the series might have offered viewers a slice of life that was too insular, too peculiar for prime time. When programmers pulled the plug, writers were finishing work on an episode starring Sammy Davis, Jr., as a Mardi Gras Indian. Incidentally, there remains no record of what tribe Davis would have belonged to, though speculation among locals was high that he would wear the headdress and feather plume of either the Wild Tchoupitoulas or Yellow Pocahontas.

the klieg lights of fame dimmed. Leslie pulled the local television ads he had been running, the ones that touted his restaurant as "the inspiration for the hit television series *Frank's Place.*" Business at the original Chez Helene stalled.

One by one, the branch locations and fried chicken franchises closed.

Already a veteran of more than twenty-five years at the
stove, Leslie shrugs off his fall from grace as if it were an Ash
Wednesday hangover. "I knew I could ride it out, that it all
would pass," he tells me. "I was still cooking, still had my little
restaurant. The real problem was that I was sitting on dyna-
mite. The dope fiends and pushers were moving into the
neighborhood. Now don't get me wrong, I know the streets.
I've lived my whole life around pimps and whores. They've
got a job to do same as me. But this was something different."

In August of 1989, Leslie declared bankruptcy. Sales taxes
were way past due. Partners with fat bankrolls and unlimited
lines of credit were long gone. In 1994 the doors closed for
good, and soon thereafter the corner building that once
housed the hottest restaurant in New Orleans burned down.
A bulldozer razed the smoke-stained yellow brick walls; three
decades of sweat and toil and garlic-perfumed grease col-
lapsed in a cloud of dust.

a nd then, like Alice down the rabbit hole, Austin Leslie
was gone. Vanished from sight. He popped up now
and again, cooking at the Basin Street Club one month, over
at the Bottom Line the next. Somewhere along the way, he
even manned the fryer at a restaurant called N'awlins just
outside of Copenhagen, Denmark. (Like a bluegrass picker
in Japan, Leslie's ego and his pocketbook required remove

from the origins of his fame.) "We had a good thing going there for a while," Leslie tells me. "They loved my gumbo. On the other hand, there's nothing like cooking Creole food in New Orleans. That's your toughest audience, your best one."

In the years since, Leslie has never really made another kitchen his own—until he answered a want ad in the New Orleans newspaper in 1996. "I think it said something like, 'Looking for a Creole/Cajun cook,'" recalls Jacques Leonardi, the elfin restauranteur who owns Jacques-Imo's. "I never thought I could get Austin to cook in a funky joint like this, but he was willing." The two men make for an odd couple: Leonardi, the joker, always ready with a drink and a slap on the back for his patrons. And Leslie, the onetime toast of New Orleans, the golden boy apparent of Creole cuisine, standing tall by the deep fryer, spearing chicken thighs from the roiling grease with an oversized carving fork.

Leslie once lorded over three restaurants and a chain of fried chicken shops. Advertising agencies plastered his smiling face on the side of New Orleans buses. Entrepreneurs heralded his story as worthy of emulation. Those days are long gone, but Leslie seems happy at Jacques-Imo's.

Since he signed on with Leonardi, Leslie has commandeered the back left corner of the kitchen. He is not the executive chef. Or the sous chef. He's the fry cook. Anything that emerges from the Keating deep fryer is his charge. Fried chicken is still his focus—and it's as garlicky good as it ever was—but Leslie now turns out some of Leonardi's more whacked creations. He's the muscle behind appetizers like deep-fried roast beef po' boys, not to mention high-wire-act entrées like Godzilla Meets Fried Green Tomato, wherein a deep-fried soft-shell crab plays the part of the monster.

Neither Leonardi's penchant for taking outsized liberties with Creole cookery, nor the swamp hut motif of Jacques-Imo's—acid sunsets airbrushed on the walls, voodoo candles on the tables, plastic alligators screwed to weathered window frames—give Leslie pause. Nowadays, he focuses his attention upon the task at hand, upon what's burbling in his deep fryer. But every couple of weeks, a reporter or savvy eater seeks him out, bent upon learning the secret of his fried chicken. Many are enticed by rumors that Leslie dips the chicken in a batter made with a brand of condensed milk that is available only in Orleans Parish. When a pilgrim presents himself and asks the question, though, Leslie just holds out his flour-covered hands for inspection, palms down then palms up. "The secret's in here," he tells them. "The secret's in here."

Creole Fried Chicken with New Orleans Confetti

NEW ORLEANS, LOUISIANA

This recipe owes its inspiration to Austin Leslie. Since he began frying chicken in the 1960s, admirers have argued over how to replicate his mastery of poultry. Unlike Willie Mae Seaton of Willie Mae's Scotch House in New Orleans, he is a devotee of deep-frying. As for Leslie's chosen ingredients, I've heard at least a dozen wild guesses, including a marinade of clam juice. Austin Leslie is part of the problem, since over the years he has given his name to a number of variations. I've tried to synthesize the best of the bunch. Though I did not embrace clam juice as a possibility, I did find that condensed milk gave the chicken a pleasant richness.

- 1 chicken weighing 3 to 4 pounds (the smaller, the better), cut into 8–10 pieces
- 2 tablespoons salt
- 2 tablespoons black pepper
- 2 tablespoons Cajun seasoning (I like Tony Chachere's.)
- 1 egg, beaten

(continued)

- 1 can (12 ounces) unsweetened condensed milk
- 1 cup water
- Peanut oil
- 1 cup all-purpose flour
- 10 slices dill pickle
- 1 garlic clove, chopped very fine
- 1 bunch parsley, chopped fine

Sprinkle salt, pepper, and Cajun seasoning over chicken and refrigerate at least 1 hour, as many as 24. Mix egg, condensed milk, and water in a bowl. Pour oil into pot to a depth of at least 3 inches and heat to 375°. Dip chicken pieces into egg wash, then dredge in flour. Shake off excess flour and slip chicken into hot oil, starting with the dark meat. Cook, maintaining a temperature of between 325° and 350°, for 12 minutes, or until an internal thermometer registers 170° for dark meat, 160° for white meat. Drain on a wire rack for 10 minutes, and garnish each piece with a pickle slice and confetti of garlic and parsley. *Serves 4.*

Coop d'Etat

When we tell the story of our country, we tend to focus on the big names, the men and women whom historians and the popular press have decreed proxies for the whole unseemly lot of us. Who won the Civil War? Abraham Lincoln. To whom do we owe the fruits of the civil rights movement? Martin Luther King, Jr.

The same applies to many of our totemic foods. We often tell the story of hamburgers by way of Ray Kroc and McDonald's, the story of hot dogs by way of a Coney Island man named Nathan. I need not remind you what name we invoke when we talk of fried chicken.

But there are a thousand other stories out there worth telling: tales of cooks who fed the civil rights movement, who fed both Confederate and Union combatants during the Civil War, who, over the course of a career, did nothing more (and nothing less) than feed their patrons skillet after skillet of peerless fried chicken. Despite his brush with fame, Austin Leslie is one of those people. And so was Lyndell Burton of Atlanta, whose story follows.

NINE

Deacon Burton and
His Atlanta Flock

he Deacon received his public while stationed at the end of the serving line, in front of the cash register. A rack of Rolaids to his right, trays of plastic cutlery to his left. And always, within arm's reach, a small brass bell, which, when Lyndell Burton required your attention, he shook with all the authority a two-inch clapper could muster.

That bell figures large in many a recollection of Deacon Burton, for it was his custom to ring it upon learning that a dignitary—or, better yet, a first-time visitor—was among the lunchtime throng at Burton's Grill. I remember my first visit. (Looking back, I now recognize it as my first pilgrimage in search of fried chicken.) The year was 1986, and I was new to Atlanta, newer still to Inman Park, the Deacon's corner of the city. "See this boy with the old knock-knees," he called out to me over the din. " We're gonna feed him some black-eyed peas."

I ate fried chicken that first day, the glories of which I had, by then, been hearing about for a good ten years. I had read about it in *Knife and Fork,* a monthly restaurant-review letter. I had seen television news reports of the Deacon's trip to Washington, D.C., to fry chicken for Congressman John Lewis. I had perused the local press tributes, wherein the writer usually managed to point out that, while Harlan Sanders was merely an honorary colonel (more than 170,000 fellow Kentuckians share the title), Lyndell Burton was an actual deacon in the Free for All Baptist Church of Decatur, Georgia. And though I can't be sure of my exact order that summer day, I imagine my lunch included a thigh and two legs, rice and gravy, black-eyed peas, and hoecakes. It became my usual, for over the next seven years, until Lyndell Burton passed away at the age of eighty-three, I was a regular.

The Deacon served chicken of a certain size. Ralph McGill, longtime editor of *The Atlanta Constitution,* described such diminutive birds as "barnyard subdebs, rarely more than ten to twelve weeks old and weighing from a pound and a half to two pounds." For me, the size of his chicken was appealing because I could order three pieces without being branded a glutton.

And, like the ladies of the Chalfonte Hotel, the Deacon served chicken of a certain softness. Though he floured his chicken and fried it in cast-iron skillets popping with grease, he did not serve birds plastered in a crust that, after two bites, fissured and fell away. His was an elastic, somehow crisp envelope that tasted of nothing more exotic than salt and pepper.

Cynics might successfully argue that other Atlantans were equally adept chicken fryers. Annie Keith, who once operated a house restaurant nearby, has her adherents. And so does Thelma Grundy of Thelma's Kitchen over near Georgia Tech. A troubling few might even look to Lester Maddox, onetime owner of the Pickrick Cafeteria, who rose to the highest office in the state by leveraging his Jim Crow–era refusal to serve fried chicken to African Americans. But Deacon Burton never claimed to serve the best in Atlanta—that title was thrust upon him. Ask him how he prepared his chicken and he'd reply, "Wash 'em, put 'em in some flour, season 'em with salt and pepper and some grease. That's all."

He was a quiet man with a thin and deeply furrowed face, a wiry body, and a smile that somehow let you know he had weathered his share of adversity. Aside from his bell-clanging habit, his only sign of ego was broadcast by his taste in hats: In his later years, the Deacon wore a high fluted chef's toque, which, when lunch service was at full tilt and the kitchen was smogged with grease, shone above the haze like a beacon. It took me a good year of sixty-second conversations at the cash register to coax forth a semblance of his life story, but I realized when I began researching this book that I still did not know nearly enough.

That's what brings me back to the Deacon's old corner today, when I take a seat at Son's Place, Lenn Storey's faithful rendering of his father's grill, I know that the boy who would become Deacon Burton was born in the town of Watkinsville, northeast of Atlanta. I know that, on a Christmas Eve when he was just fourteen, Burton ran away from home. I know that by Christmas Day he found work as a dishwasher at Faust, a Greek restaurant in downtown Atlanta.

Burton rose from dishwasher to cook, working at some of the best Atlanta dining rooms of the day, including those of the Henry Grady Hotel and the Capital City Club. And I know that Burton cooked in the Navy during World War II, feeding three meals a day to 4,000 men. He opened Burton's Grill after returning home from the war, and in the early years moved it from a highway north of town to Inman Park.

Lenn Storey and I talk over his father's and his own cooking career. Growing up, Storey did not know Burton was his father, but he was already following in his footsteps, first, during high school, pressure-frying chicken in a Kentucky Fried Chicken–licensed cafeteria, and later, when he cooked communal meals for his fellow Atlanta firemen. We talk of the time just after his father's death when Storey fought a bitter and ultimately unsuccessful court battle to legally establish his lineage. And we talk of the first time that the Deacon rang the brass bell and announced to all in attendance, "I want y'all to meet my boy, my son, Lenn Storey."

a s we talk, I gnaw on a plate of Lenn Storey's chicken. It tastes like I remember his father's chicken tasting. Nothing fancy here, just salt and pepper and schmaltz. (That's schmaltz as originally employed in the Yiddish language, meaning not maudlin sentimentality, but chicken fat.) And the restaurant, which sits cheek-to-jowl with his father's old corner storefront (now converted to an Italian trattoria), is a dead ringer for Burton's Grill. As I eat, I grow sentimental. Even the serving line, outfitted with those light green melamine lunch trays, conjures his father's spirit. But what Storey may never conjure is the spirit of the times in which Deacon Burton came to be a revered cook, a beloved Atlantan. And in many ways, he would not want to.

When many whites first discovered Burton's Grill in the 1970s, fried chicken was considered a relic of days gone by, back before the civil rights movement, maybe even before the Civil War. At Aunt Fanny's Cabin, a restaurant out in the suburb of Smyrna, fried chicken was presented as the ultimate plantation dish, a savory of step-and-fetch-it allure served to locals and tourists alike amidst the retrograde splendor of a retrofitted slave lodging. Downtown, at Pittypat's Porch (named for a character in *Gone With the Wind*), the trappings were more tasteful, but the underlying message was no less offensive.

Burton's Grill was different. Black Atlantans had long doted on Paschal's Restaurant, on what was then called Hunter Street, taking pride in the fact that some of the seminal events in the civil rights movement, including the 1965 Selma-to-Montgomery march, were planned over platters of their fried chicken. But for many whites that proud history proved intimidating.

In time—no one seems to know how or why—everyone seems to have made their way over to Burton's Grill. It may well have been the first Atlanta restaurant where the food and the setting inspired blacks and whites to recognize their common humanity across a table set with fried chicken and black-eyed peas and cornbread. Though it was black-owned, it somehow came to be considered comparatively neutral ground. Many locals remember Burton's Grill as one of the first places where they saw blacks and whites interacting without nervous pomp or pretense. And all—black and white—remember the first time they visited, the first time a kindly gentleman rang a small brass bell and, above the report of the clapper, shouted out a welcome.

Deep South Deacon-Fried Chicken

ATLANTA, GEORGIA

Deacon Burton was a minimalist. I don't suppose he would have approved of my use of thyme. His spice cabinet was bare except for a tin of black pepper, a box of salt. But I am a mere mortal, not able to coax from chicken the stupendous flavor for which the Deacon was known. Herewith, my tribute to the Deacon, my heretical stab at transcendence.

- 1 chicken weighing 3 to 4 pounds (the smaller, the better), cut into 8–10 pieces
- 8 teaspoons salt
- 1 quart cold water
- 4 teaspoons black pepper
- 4 teaspoons thyme
- 1 cup self-rising flour
- Lard, or shortening into which you mix about 3 tablespoons bacon grease

Dissolve 4 teaspoons of the salt in the cold water and soak chicken in water for 1 hour. Drain and then pat almost dry. Season chicken with 2 teaspoons each of the

(continued)

salt and pepper, and 2 teaspoons of the thyme. Mix flour and remaining 2 teaspoons each of the salt, pepper, and thyme in a heavy paper or plastic bag. Add a couple of pieces of chicken at a time, shake to coat thoroughly, and shake again upon removal to loosen excess flour. Remove floured chicken to a wax-paper- or parchment-lined pan. Refrigerate if you plan to wait more than 10 minutes to fry.

Heat lard or shortening over medium-high in a cast-iron skillet, to reach a depth of 1½ inches when liquefied. When the liquid reaches 350°, slip the dark meat in, skin-side down, followed by the white meat. Keep the lard or shortening between 300° and 325° and cook each side for 5–6 minutes covered and then 5–6 minutes uncovered, for a total of 20–24 minutes, or until an internal thermometer registers 170° for dark meat, 160° for white meat. Drain on a wire rack, blotting with paper towels as necessary. *Serves 3 or 4.*

It Takes a Village to Fry a Chicken

I have long been fascinated by the shoebox lunch, a traveler's repast assembled in a box that once contained high heels with grosgrain bows or brogans studded with brass eyelets. As constructed by a mother, an aunt, or a family cook, it might hold a fried chicken leg, a half-sandwich of pimento cheese on crustless white, a couple of deviled eggs tucked in a sleeve of wax paper. And, secreted away from the prying eyes and appetites of neighbors, it might even include a slice of red velvet cake slicked with cream cheese icing.

Until recently, as a self-aware and somewhat defensive native of the South, I thought of shoebox lunches as harbingers of the bad ol' days. They conjured a time when laws and customs complicated a trip of any distance in the Jim Crow South, dictating that black citizens could not eat alongside white. But, in the story that follows, the story of the railroad cooks of Gordonsville, Virginia, I found a story of black and white interaction and eating on the go in which I might eke out a measure of pride.

TEN

The Chicken Bone Express

the creosote-swabbed timbers of the CSX rail trestle loom large at a bend in the road leading into Gordonsville, Virginia, a small town twenty-five miles north of Charlottesville. Even today, the sight and sound of a locomotive heaving up and over the trestle, skirting town at rooftop height, commands attention. The brute force of the engine calls to mind the days when Gordonsville was the junction of the Chesapeake & Ohio and the Orange, Alexandria & Manassas.

Catercorner from the trestle is an abandoned freight depot. Beyond that is the two-story clapboard Exchange Hotel, commandeered as a Confederate hospital during the Civil War and now home to a museum dedicated to the late unpleasantness. Across the way—and of greatest import for the purposes of my fried chicken quest—is the onetime site of Gordonsville's passenger station. That's where, from the mid-1800s until at least the 1930s, African American women peddled food to travelers whose trains stopped here to take on water and coal.

Gordonsville was not the sole town that fostered such entrepreneurial activity. Natives of Corinth, a onetime railroad town in northeastern Mississippi, tell tales of Julia Brown, who in 1867—just two years after gaining status as a freedwoman—began meeting trains at the depot, selling drumsticks and wings. Ditto long-tenured residents of Philadelphia, Pennsylvania, who speak fondly of the kerchiefed women who greeted new arrivals at Reading Terminal with baskets of tissue-wrapped thighs priced at a nickel per piece.

These women came of age when rail lines had not yet adopted the niceties of service that came to define midtwentieth-century travel. There were no Pullman car berths for overnight passage. No dining cars boasted tables napped with linen and set with crystal and china. Instead, as Barbara Haber revealed in her recent book *From Hardtack to Home Fries*, in 1857 *The New York Times* reported that many travelers endured long days, with "hot cinders flying in their faces" before approaching a station "dying with weariness, hunger, and thirst, longing for an opportunity to bathe their faces at least before partaking of their much-needed refreshments. . . . The consequence of such savage and unnatural feeding are not reported by telegraph as railroad disasters; but if a faithful account were taken of them we are afraid they would be found much more serious than any that are caused by the smashing of cars, or the breaking of bridges."

The African American women of Gordonsville were among the first entrepreneurs to define and satisfy the nutritional needs of travelers. Without a doubt, thousands of other women, in hundreds of other towns, tried their hand at the same. (My colleague Psyche Williams-Forson has written a dissertation on the subject of black women and chicken, *Building Houses out of Chicken Legs*.) But a peculiar confluence of capitalistic hustle, booming rail traffic, and proximity to the media outlets of nearby Washington, D.C., gave rise to Gordonsville's unmatched reputation for poultry cookery. Indeed, by 1869, essayist George W. Bagby was calling the town "the chicken-leg centre of the universe." It was a title to which the city would lay claim long after the last Gordonsville train boarded passengers.

Visiting Gordonsville, I take stock of the legacy of those cooks, talking to their descendants and admirers. Key to my visit is the afternoon I pass in the company of octogenarians Mildred and Pete Avery. Mr. Avery's mother, Elsie Swift, and her sister, Mamie Swift, were veterans of the local fried chicken trade, and were, along with their fellow townspeople, known as waiter-carriers. The moniker may have come from their practice of *carrying* trays of chicken and pie and coffee from their homes to the train platform where they would *wait* on passengers.

Over the course of the afternoon, I learn much about the *idea* of waiter-carriers. I begin to understand that the frying of chicken was a step toward independence for African American women during the dark days when labor and the products of labor were the property of slaveholders. Talking with Pete—who recalls plucking the chickens his mother and aunt killed and scalded—I realize that these women were employing a sort of vertical business integration, raising fryers from chicks, feeding them out to a weight of two or three pounds, and then cooking them and serving them to travelers. It was an early and important underground economy that leveraged self-reliance and rewarded its practitioners with an independence that many of their sharecropping husbands could not muster.

Pete tells me of the seemingly superhuman strength of those waiter-carriers. They were able, he says, to muscle a tray stacked with baskets of fried chicken and pots of coffee above their heads, to carry them from home kitchens to the station. They would heft them again when a train arrived, so that customers leaning from passenger coach windows might reach down and serve themselves. When I hear Pete talk of the beautiful dresses the women wore beneath their starched white aprons, and the multicolored hats they donned to cover bandanna-clad heads, I imagine a band of regal women in whom the whole community might take great pride.

When Pete describes the preparation of chicken—how the birds benefited from two soaks in salted water and how the women battered them with water and flour and fried them in locally rendered lard—my mouth waters for a taste of bird as prepared in the Gordonsville style. But luck is not with me. It seems that the last of the businesses connected to the trade, Hattie's Inn, closed a while back. And while Pete's wife, Mildred, does fry chicken in the traditional Gordonsville manner, she does so—on order from Pete's doctor—just one day a week. Since that day is Wednesday and my audience with the Avery family takes place on a Thursday, I am, for the moment, out of luck. (I did, upon returning home, develop a Gordonsville style recipe based on Pete's description and a few tricks of my own; turn to page 104.)

i don't know why no progeny came forward to carry on the tradition, after the Swift family stowed their trays, when Hattie closed her doors. (I am reminded again of Calvin Trillin's observation that "a superior fried-chicken restaurant is often the institutional extension of a single chicken-obsessed woman . . . it is not easily passed down intact.") When I query Pete, he just mumbles about changing times. He is similarly inscrutable when I ask why the Gordonsville Fried Chicken Festival, established in June of 2001, has failed to garner strong support from the local African American community.

But after pondering these developments for a while, I believe I may have tentative answers. The matter of the annual festival is simplest. Some locals see it as a grand ruse staged to ferret out the fried chicken recipes perfected long ago by the waiter-carriers. That may be a bit harsh, but, to my mind, the festival—driven by tourism funds and executed by the local visitors' bureau—fails to pay appropriate homage to the waiter-carriers. Maybe before you can pay tribute to these women, you must first acknowledge that they thrived at the margins, beyond the gaze of the city fathers, taking pride in a sort of renegade capitalism that was quite the opposite of a city-sponsored event.

This distrust of officialdom is deep-rooted. Many have posited that the waiter-carriers met their demise as trains modernized, first adding dining cars, then closing carriages and restricting easy passenger access to the foods vended by the women, and finally, in the 1930s and 1940s, introducing air-conditioning and sealing the carriages. But there are others who believe that the real culprits were local laws and sanctions that appear on the books as early as 1879, when the city fathers began to grasp the impact of the waiter-carriers, and the town council began requiring snack vendors' licenses, and collecting a tax thereon.

This alternate explanation gains strength when I find a 1970 interview from the local newspaper with Bella Watson, described as the sole surviving waiter-carrier. The article refers obliquely to early struggles for vending franchises that exiled waiter-carriers to the opposite side of the tracks from the platform. The eighty-year-old does not mince words about the end of the era. "There was a health officer from Richmond," she recalls. "I still remember his name, but I won't say it. [He] used to make me so mad that sometimes I would cuss and sometimes I would cry. They made us wrap our chicken in oilpaper and even wanted to see where we cooked it. Of course, we had our secret ways of cooking that chicken and I believe he just wanted to find that out."

A cynic might say that little has changed in the intervening thirty-odd years: the powers that be still want that recipe. But I'm not *quite* that cynical. On the contrary, it seems good—even just—that fifty years after the era of the waiter-carriers has passed, the fried chicken recipes perfected by those early entrepreneurs are still in demand. I find hope in the knowledge that a new generation of Virginians considers such treasures to be matters of private concern, of family dowry, known only to women like Mildred Avery.

Trackside Fried Chicken Destined for a Shoebox Lunch

GORDONSVILLE, VIRGINIA

Battered chicken has long been popular south of the Mason-Dixon, and this is my recipe inspired by the waiter-carriers of Gordonsville, Virginia. Try it hot from the skillet, or cooled to room temperature and ferried to a picnic table by a basket or a shoebox. Better yet, eat the first batch, and then fry a second batch to eat cold, after an overnight in the fridge.

- 1 chicken weighing 3 to 4 pounds (the smaller, the better), cut into 8–10 pieces
- 1½ cups all-purpose flour
- 1 tablespoon salt
- 1 tablespoon black pepper
- 1 tablespoon paprika
- 2 tablespoons ground sage
- 2 cups 2% milk
- 1 egg, beaten
- Peanut oil into which you mix about 3 tablespoons bacon grease

Combine 1 cup of the flour, the salt, pepper, paprika, and 1 tablespoon of the sage in a bowl. Stir in milk and beaten egg to make a thin batter. Roll chicken in remaining flour. Dip chicken into batter one piece at a time. Shake off excess batter. Place chicken on wire rack and let stand in refrigerator for 15 minutes. Heat oil, at a depth of 3 inches, to 350°. Add chicken skin-side down, and cook uncovered at 325° for 8–12 minutes per side, or until an internal thermometer registers 170° for dark meat, 160° for white meat. Drain on wire rack. Sprinkle with remaining sage. *Serves 4.*

Good Preacher Gone Bad

fried chicken eating and churchgoing are long intertwined. I uncovered three examples of the synergy while on the research trail:

■ At the Whole Truth Church and Lunchroom, a church-run enterprise in Wilson, North Carolina, funds are raised from the sale of fried chicken and collard greens. The money pays for the closed–circuit audio broadcasts that beam in the good word of the reigning bishop in the Church of the Lord Jesus Christ of the Apostolic Faith.

■ Given an audience with a good sense of humor and an appreciation of liturgical pomp, you can make the case that the beauty of a golden breast of fried chicken emerging from the depths of a pot burbling with oil has its roots in the Pentecostal tendency to dismiss a baptismal sprinkle in favor of full immersion.

■ And for the purposes of advancing this narrative, you should know that, at St. Paul's Catholic Church in New Alsace, Indiana, annual fried chicken dinners (an account of which follows) replenish the congregation's coffers and foster fellowship that envelops the whole of the community.

But keep in mind that the relationship between church and chicken also has its downside. Psyche Williams-Forson once told me that there are four things that can bring a preacher down. She calls them the four C's: cash, chicks, Cadillacs, and chicken. Fried chicken, to be specific. Too much praise of one sister's cooking tells the congregation that the preacher is availing himself of more than her gospel bird.

ELEVEN

Chasing Chicken
on a Slow Time
Sunday Morning

t's just past nine on a Sunday morning when I roll into the burg of New Alsace, Indiana. The drive west from Cincinnati, Ohio, took less than an hour, but the change is remarkable. After threading my way through strip malls and burger boxes, the Indiana countryside is a balm. As the highway narrows to two lanes, roadside billboards advertising discount denture fabricators give way, and plywood signs tacked to fence posts emerge, heralding a community quilt sale, an antique tractor show.

Even the telling of time is different here. While the great majority of the country adheres to Daylight Saving Time, the rural precincts of Indiana, in deference to farmers who start their workday early, do not fiddle with their clocks. They prefer instead to hold steady year-round to what they call slow time.

I arrive intent upon surveying the Catholic-parish chicken dinners staged throughout the Midwest. From what I was able to glean before I hit the road, Ohio and contiguous states appear to be at the epicenter of the phenomenon. Beginning in May and continuing through early November, more than fifty churches in the three-state region host dinners. Traditionally, the source for a roster of dates and churches was word of mouth or an advertisement in the *Catholic Telegraph Register,* but, as with all aspects of modern American life, the Internet has recently made inroads. Since 1996, fried chicken devotee Carl Heilmann of the University of Cincinnati has operated a web database of dinners, www.thinkingchicken.com.

With Carl's help, I chose the second weekend in August for my expedition, because, with a good map and a bit of dispatch, I might be able to sample three dinners in three different states in one day. The plan we devised was that I would hit New Alsace early, then forge on to parishes in Ohio and Kentucky. Even though I would eventually succeed in my three-part quest, I knew as I drove through the rutted field alongside St. Paul's burying ground that I could curtail my investigations and be utterly content at New Alsace. I had a feeling, as the soaring brick sanctuary came into view, that the food would prove to be that good, the community bonds that compelling.

t wo hours before the first chicken dinner is served at eleven a.m., the St. Paul church grounds are already abuzz with activity. Out front, beneath a tent on loan from an undertaker, a clutch of men hunches over an oversized gaming wheel, making adjustments to ensure a proper advantage for the house. One tent over, a teenage girl counts out raffle tickets that entitle winners to a slab of bacon or a rosy ham.

Around back, a crew of three women staffs a country store. There you can purchase a pair of Wolverine boots from which sprout entangled tendrils of wandering Jew, as well as ingots of zucchini-pineapple-walnut bread, sealed in rose-tinted plastic wrap. Beneath the boughs of an elm tree, a middle-aged woman in a smock shoves a chair into place for her husband, the dealer who will preside over a church-sponsored game of what is known locally as giant poker. Soon he will slide legal-pad-sized cards to beer-drinking players with a quarter or three riding on each hand.

As a son of the Protestant South, raised in proximity to all manner of Baptists, these vignettes of Catholic parish life confound me. But they don't scare me. On the contrary, after enduring years of punch-and-cookie socials, I may have found my people.

i n the kitchen, beneath the adjacent schoolhouse, I meet eighty-something-year-old Tillie Hoffbauer, whose smiling face is framed by a cumulus of white curls. Though my goal is to get a bead on the fried chicken cooking tradition hereabouts, and I know that Tillie's expertise is in the preparation of dressing, I can't resist an audience with her. I'm rewarded with an early morning taste of that dressing, rich with stock made from chicken necks and stoked with bounteous quantities of week-old white bread.

The dressing does not disappoint. And neither does the mock turtle soup or the fried chicken livers I sample from the cook tent pitched just beyond her kitchen door. But I keep my appetite in check. The crew of fry cooks are setting up their kettles beyond the blacktop parking lot, beneath a tight arbor of oak trees. I hope to be able to both eat my fill and come to know how and why the tradition of parish picnics has thrived in New Alsace since at least the 1890s.

For a good fifteen minutes I amble about, introducing myself to any of the twenty-odd cooks who will meet my gaze and suffer my queries. Then I latch on to Jim Sublett, a craggy-faced tool-and-die maker from nearby Cedar Grove. Jim and his son Don work a fryer crafted from an old cast-iron wash pot, sheathed in an insulating jacket of castoff piping, and fired by a burner salvaged from a household furnace.

When I ask Jim about the history of St. Paul's chicken dinner feed, he stops me midsentence. "I'm not a member of this church," he says above the throaty hiss of the oil-filled kettles. "I'm not even Catholic. We just come to hang out with the cooks and do our part. We fry at four of these dinners every summer; for the fire department, for the Catholics, it's all the same to us."

Jim's comments prove to be a recurring theme of my New Alsace explorations. These people are not grandstanders. Here, the doing of good deeds is considered a privilege, not a duty. That is not to say that they are saints-in-training: One of the cooks, a barrel-gutted man in his late twenties, wearing a T-shirt that advertises his prowess in horseshoe tossing, seems still drunk from the night before. When he lurches hard against a tree while dropping a load of chicken into his kettle, a fellow cook hands him a beer in an attempt to restore his liquid equilibrium.

before the morning is over and the wait to gain admittance to the gymnasium-cum-dining-room swells to more than an hour, I buy a ticket and take a seat at one of the folding tables arranged, with military precision, on the basketball court. While seated, I eat a surfeit of fried chicken hemmed in a pepper-flecked parchment of crust. I inhale a thatch of bacon-napped coleslaw. I nibble at mashed potatoes that began the day as a mound of dehydrated flakes. I blanket Tillie's dressing in a gush of cracklin'-studded gravy and dig my fork deep.

I even have the opportunity to engage table captain Donna

Huff, who has served here for thirty-seven consecutive years. Her great-great-grandfather's niece—whose name Donna cannot recall but a historian of New Alsace records as Mary Even—was one of the originators of the tradition. As Donna mediates squabbles over a dwindling supply of pineapple upside-down cake, she tells me that the annual dinner now draws more than two thousand people and nets the church tens of thousands of dollars. This big event had its beginnings in the ice cream social craze of the Victorian era. Mary Even organized socials to raise money for the church; she and her sisters and cousins solicited buckets of cream from local dairy farmers, and blocks of ice from local saloons, to make the confection.

When I'm done, I pine for a return to the cook tents. Word has it that, after three or four batches of chicken, the oil becomes impregnated with sufficient schmaltz and salt and pepper to render a product that far surpasses what I ate during my early luncheon.

Jim Sublett is where I left him, perched over a kettle of chicken. Above him floats a nimbus of grease and steam. Arrayed behind him, in front of him, are twenty-six other kettles. St. Joseph's parishioners tend some. Community volunteers like Jim and Don tend others. All appreciate the camaraderie and the chance to snack on fried gizzards or sneak a pinch from the plastic tubs of Tillie's dressing which, every half-hour or so, a young boy lugs from the kitchen and hefts onto a makeshift buffet fashioned from a stump, a chair bottom, a cooler.

When, after fifteen minutes or so of immersion, Jim's chicken bobs to the surface, he scoops the sandy-brown pieces from the kettle, and, after a brief shake, deposits the chicken in a speckle-ware dishpan at his feet. Soon, a runner will come by to ferry his birds into the dining room. While he waits, Jim dips into the burbling grease for any cracklin's that might burn and render his oil acrid.

He drops the nuggets of fused chicken fat into an over-sized tin can, which a second team of runners will eventually empty for use in the gravy. I watch his progress, waiting for the moment when the cracklin's have cooled enough to palm. By this time, I have commandeered the makings of a fine midday snack: a paper plate heaped with dressing, a brace of deep-fried gizzards, and an ice-cold Old Style beer snagged from a fellow fryer's cooler.

In the distance, I can hear the trill of a toy train whistle, the clack of the betting wheel, the splinter-voiced call of teenage boys hawking raffle tickets for baby blankets and twenty-five-dollar savings bonds. I settle into a squat alongside Jim's fryer and scoop a ragged hunk of dressing from my plate, which now rests on a patch of grease-soaked ground. Jim pulls another load from the fryer and asks me to mind his gear while he takes a bathroom break. I nod, and in so doing, take my first, tentative step from interloper to acolyte in the brotherhood of fry cooks.

Fried Chicken Cooked
in the Great Out-of-Doors

n o recipe follows this chapter because, in large part, the secret to St. Paul's fried chicken has less to do with recipe and technique and more to do with where the chicken is cooked: out of doors.

Though you can buy a ready-made kit of the type marketed for crawfish boils and turkey fries, I recommend a homegrown rig much like the one Jim Sublett uses: a propane-fueled fryer set within a cast-iron sleeve. Mine is of sufficient circumference that when I heft up my cast-iron washpot (a flea-market prize) it cradles within quite snugly. Equipped with an oversized seine purchased at a restaurant supply house and four quarts of peanut oil, I'm ready to tackle any of these recipes that call for deep frying.

And my wife appreciates the fact that the oil perfumes our backyard instead of our kitchen.

Chicken Little

C hicken wings came to the fore in the 1980s. Their arrival at corner taverns and national chain eateries compelled a reexamination of the anatomical composition of what zoologists know as *Gallus domesticus*.

It was a transitional time in the evolution of chicken terminology. The popularity of wishbones—known more often in rural areas as pulleybones, dubbed merrythoughts in England—was on the wane (though the term had yet to be resigned to recognition as a brand of salad dressing or an offensive football formation). For the record, the wishbone is the forked structure in front of the chicken's breastbone, formed by the fusion of the clavicles. According to widely embraced superstition, when two people tug at the ends of a wishbone, the person who retains the longer piece is granted a wish.

But enough of the old lingo. Buffalo chicken wings demanded the dissemination of new terms: tips, flats, and drums. Soon we knew that the proper preparation of chicken wings called for the cook to snip off the tips and cut the remaining wings into meager-fleshed flats (comprising the ulna and radius) and drums (the meaty humerus). Even if we did not immediately warm to the new terminology, we learned that a flat didn't taste fine unless you fried it to a crisp, lavished it with hot sauce, and dragged it through a cup of blue cheese dressing.

TWELVE

On the Wings
of Mother Teressa

buffalo, New York, is a drinking man's town. And, despite what detractors will tell you about the year-round threat of blizzards at this outpost on the Canadian border, ice-cold beer seems to be the preferred drink of most Buffalo men. In preparation for my summer sojourn there, I read a number of texts, including Dale Anderson and Bob Riley's opus *A Beer Drinker's Guide to Buffalo Bars;* Verlyn Klinkenborg's homage to his father-in-law's Buffalo tavern, *The Last Fine Time;* and, more to the point, Calvin Trillin's *New Yorker* essay "An Attempt to Compile a Short History of the Buffalo Chicken Wing."

To further get myself in the proper frame of mind, I read each while seated at a bar near my Oxford, Mississippi, home, swilling drafts and snarfing down wing after spicy wing. I ate the chicken in a rather halfhearted stab at research, while I drank the beer to cool the fire and brighten my mood; for I did not begin my examination of Buffalo chicken wings eagerly.

I tried my best to avoid the subject of Buffalo chicken wings. I even pondered a polemic in favor of restoring the beef-on-weck sandwich to its rightful stature as the region's signature food. The genesis of my plaint was multifaceted. Blame media and menu saturation. Blame my tendency to embrace the singular, the fleeting: to deify the whale-blubber-fried chicken that I have not yet tasted but have heard tell is cooked on the occasion of a full moon, on an oil derrick that straddles the Bering Strait.

But how could I deny that, based upon the parameters set for this book, Buffalo wings are an iconic example of fried chicken? They have a bone. (Flats even have two.) They attain their crunch by way of immersion in roiling oil. And a hell of a lot of people know them as the quintessential bar food.

S o it is that I find myself in Buffalo, thinking big thoughts like, *Who has the right to declare any city to be a capital of anything?* By my reckoning, it's an enterprise best left to historians backed by a retinue of fierce graduate students, chamber of commerce types absent any sense of propriety, or interlopers like me equipped with nothing save a bit of perspective. Accordingly, it should come as no surprise that, thirty minutes into my Buffalo expedition, I make the bold decision to enshrine this post-industrial city—along with Nashville, Tennessee, and Kansas City, Missouri (about which you will learn more in succeeding chapters)—in my pantheon of fried chicken capitals.

This insight comes to me as I pilot my rental car down a wide Buffalo boulevard, alternately digging into a box of medium-hot wings and wiping excess sauce on my jeans. I pass Duff's, a onetime Mexican restaurant that switched over from tacos to wings long ago; two Chinese buffeterias that boast strong sub-specialties in teriyaki and barbecue wings; a sandwich shop that, based upon the special that blinks forth from tonight's menu board, may well do the same; and a hospital which, in seeming anticipation of the dawning of the age of the Buffalo chicken wing, installed the first cardiac pacemaker implant in 1960.

When I stop at a traffic light, a Ford with a Domino's Pizza sign fixed to the roof pulls alongside. It is driven by a kid who—and I swear this is gospel—flicks a wing out his window, watches as it bounces off the blacktop, dabs sauce from his lips with the sleeve of his uniform, and, as the light changes to green, speeds away. Soon after I recover enough to proceed, I look up to see a restaurant sign looming in the distance. The place is called Just Pizza, but even these good folks can't leave well enough alone. According to the advertisements blazoned on the front window, they sell wings too.

By the time I reach the Anchor Bar, I have passed more than a dozen chicken wing vendors. I stopped at three, of which Duff's is my current favorite, if only because they are generous with their blue cheese dressing. I remind myself that I have much further to go, that I'm only at the Anchor Bar to set a sort of baseline for my study of Buffalo wings. But two steps into the vestibule and I'm a goner. Truth be told, I am predisposed to like any place that stakes its reputation for great music on the vocal stylings of a woman named Miss Dodo Greene. What's more, I did not anticipate the import of treading the same duckboards where a dish was conceived.

Imagine finding the first baker of apple pie. She's been dead for centuries. How about the first cook to stuff a broiled meat patty between two slices of bread? True believers will still be squabbling over the inventor of the hamburger when the Southern Baptist Convention elects its first openly gay leader. But here, at the 1940 vintage Anchor Bar, a vaguely Italianate warehouse on a forlorn street south of downtown, one can pull up a stool, order a beer, and pay homage to the maker amidst the trappings of a true cathedral of creation.

I did not arrive in Buffalo unawares. My readings, and forty years of pop acculturation, had equipped me with the basics, the tenets of the chicken wing catechism as handed down by the Bellissimo family, longtime proprietors of the

Anchor Bar. I knew that, among aficionados, there is little to no squabbling over the year, 1964, in which Buffalo chicken wings were conceived. But I also knew that devotees tell a number of contradictory stories of the evening in question. The two most often cited are these:

■ Teressa Bellissimo invented Buffalo chicken wings when her son Dominic and a cadre of friends came by the bar in search of a late-night snack. Teressa rescued a mess of wings intended for the stockpot, cut them in half, cooked them to a crisp, and sprinkled the wings with hot sauce before serving them with a bowl of blue cheese dressing and a few strips of celery swiped from an antipasto platter.

■ The impetus was the Catholic prohibition against eating meat on Friday. As the clock inched toward midnight on a Friday, Dominic asked his mother to prepare something special for the Saturday-morning revelers. Again she crisped said wings and swiped said celery and added a monkey bowl of blue cheese for good measure.

I also knew that there exists an heretical story that does not involve Teressa Bellissimo. Among certain hard-shell Anchor Bar devotees, the claim of primacy by John Young, onetime proprietor of a Buffalo take-away shop called Wings 'n' Things, stirs the same sort of ire that tales of Sally Hemings's lineage precipitate among myopic descendants of Thomas Jefferson.

Many serious eaters dismiss his claim when they learn that Young neither clipped nor disjointed his wings, that he had the audacity to batter them before frying, and that his hot sauce (known to patrons as mambo sauce) was based upon a honey-mustard-cayenne mix instead of a margarine-cayenne blend. Those inconsistencies did not stop me, however, from driving seventy-five miles from Buffalo to Rochester, searching for an analogue to Wings 'n' Things in the locally revered mini-chain known as Sal's Birdland. What's more, Young's tale later compelled a visit to Washington, D.C., where Buffalo newspaperwoman Janice Okun reported that Young got the idea for mambo sauce. To this day, D.C. take-aways like Yum's serve mambo-drenched wings to the demimonde. But I digressed then, and I digress now.

the decor of the Anchor Bar calls to mind an *Antiques Roadshow* prop room overseen by a drunk with impeccable taste in late-twentieth-century detritus. Unlike bars where the manager hangs a red wagon and a rusted Coca-Cola sign from the ceiling in an attempt to create what his franchise manual terms "a mood," the Anchor Bar comes by it honestly with castoff softball trophies, Statue of Liberty sculptures, crab traps, and out-of-state license plates.

Ivano Toscano occupies a stool in the corner. He is a pug of a man, a first-generation immigrant who was born in Italy and made his way here after falling for a Yugoslavian beauty he met at a nudist beach. Ivano wears a watch fashioned from gold nuggets; his shirt pocket sports a cellophane-wrapped cigar. With the death of Frank and Teressa Bellisimo and the retirement of subsequent Anchor Bar scions, he is the major-domo of wingdom.

We shake hands, and I brace for the onslaught. I expect Ivano to loose a harangue on the virtues of Anchor Bar chicken wings. But he is mercifully free of any predilection to speechify, and I don't risk my luck by prodding.

Instead, I follow his lead and order a beer. And then another. We talk of chicken wings now and again, but we also talk of politics and women and baseball. It's late afternoon, and the pace of the bar quickens. Ivano watches the door, and I watch the crowd, my eyes alert, my pen at the ready. I'm intent upon recording for posterity one of those vignettes which, in the retelling, allow a writer to encapsulate the whole of an experience.

No such vignettes present themselves. I order a basket of hot wings. And I ponder a number of questions: *Is this the first food of mass appeal invented in the television age? Is this the sole dish of the twentieth century that has its origins in offal?* But I do not break the spell by asking these questions of Ivan. Instead, I eat my basket of hot wings. The vapors swirling upward from the pile tickle and then inflame my nostrils. The wings taste no better, no worse, than any of the others I will eat over the next few days.

Ivano and I order another beer. High on the barback, I spy a miniature chicken bucket filled with the plastic chits and playing cards necessary to play a round of what was once heralded as the country's newest game sensation, the Buffalo-Style Chicken Game. Behind me, I hear one fellow exclaim to his barmate, "Hey, that guy has a pad and pen—I wonder if he works for the TV station." On the far wall, I glimpse an oil portrait of the Italian explorer Amerigo Vespucci.

When I rise to depart for the bathroom, Ivano stands too. He has caught sight of a development that requires his attention. In his left hand he now holds a cordless power drill, outfitted with a Phillips-head screwdriver. A man walks toward him, bearing a Wisconsin license plate. The man is positively radiant. He appears to be a pilgrim like me, overjoyed at the prospect of being in the very spot where the chicken wing was invented. On second thought, maybe, like me, he's just drunk. I cannot understand a word he says, but Ivano can. And as the man prattles on in Italian, Ivano screws his car tag to a place of honor alongside the waitress station.

Buffalo Wings (Prepared in an Almost Reverential Manner)

BUFFALO, NEW YORK

Local lore holds that Teressa Bellissimo originally crisped her wings in an oven. Lucky she switched to the deep-fryer, or she would have never made this book. Worshipers at the church of the Anchor will damn my cornstarch crust as heretical, but it improves the all-important crunch. Speaking of which, to maintain that crunch, do not toss wings with the hot sauce until serving.

- 24 chicken wings (about 4 pounds), tips removed and remaining wings separated into drums and flats
- ¼ cup cornstarch
- ¼ cup all-purpose flour
- 2 tablespoons black pepper
- 1 tablespoon paprika (the hot kind, if you can find it)
- Peanut oil
- ¼ stick butter

(continued)

- 1 clove garlic, minced
- ½ cup Louisiana brand hot sauce (or any viscous hot sauce)

Mix cornstarch, flour, pepper, and paprika in a paper bag. Toss in wings 6 at a time and shake to coat evenly. Pour oil in a deep and heavy pot to a depth of 3 inches. Heat oil to 350°. Fry the wings in batches of 6 or 8 or so until firm, approximately 8 minutes. They may still be a bit blond, but their edges will be russet. Skein wings from oil and place on wire rack to drain. Place butter and garlic in metal bowl; pour the hot sauce over and heat over low until the butter melts and the sauce is combined. Toss wings in the bowl to coat, and remove with a skein. Serve with celery sticks and a dressing of blue cheese mixed with sour cream, a bit of chopped garlic, and a splash of aromatic vinegar. *Serves 6 as an appetizer or 2 as a snack with beer.*

Why Didn't I Think of That?

If imitation is the sincerest form of flattery, then what are we to make of the culinary riff?

I'm thinking of dishes that, in their naming, in their construction, in their reason for being, tip a metaphorical hat to the first man or woman to slather marshmallow fluff between two cookies, cover the sandwich in a vanilla fondant, and pronounce the resulting confection to be a Moon Pie. I'm thinking of dishes that pay sly homage to the creator of the corn dog by way of a stick-mounted lobe of foie gras, encased in a cornmeal jacket and served with a chalice of cherries jubilee.

When I think of poultry riffs, I think of the deep-fried duck wings served with a sauce of fermented black beans and chilies at Le Zinc in lower Manhattan. More prosaically, if no less reverently, I think of the fried chicken that Union Square Café chef Michael Romano developed for its sister restaurant, Blue Smoke. I think of the time I spent in his kitchen as he summoned forth recollections of the chicken served at Gus's in Mason, Tennessee, as he doctored up batter until he got as close as New York palates will allow. Michael's recipe is on page 135, immediately following the story of Gus's and other Tennessee fryers of spicy birds.

THIRTEEN

The Bouglean Conceit

Something nags at me as I munch a capsicum-dusted breast at Mr. Boo's Fried Chicken in suburban Nashville, Tennessee. And it's not my cholesterol count. It's the story proprietor Diana Bouglea tells about how her chicken owes its heat to a pepper grown only in Poteet Parish, Louisiana. While she sketches a portrait of the plantation down south of I-10 to which the Bouglea family returns each August for the pepper harvest, I call forth a mental map of south Louisiana and begin ticking off parish names: La Fourche, Terrebone, Assumption, Iberville, Iberia, Vermilion. I know my list is just a start, but I swear I've never heard of Poteet.

I ask her to spell the parish name. I have it right. I ask again, just to be sure that my suspicion is not borne of faulty translation, and she points to the whiteboard above the counter where someone has scrawled, "Our business is all about the Bouglea pepper, grown on the Bouglea farm in Poteet Parish, Louisiana." Instead of pressing the point, I take another bite of chicken, stifling a sneeze as my nose grazes the crisp, Bouglea-coated crust.

When I return to my car and unfold an official-issue Louisiana road map, I scan the list of parishes. There is no Poteet Parish. But instead of marching back in and demanding a correction, I chalk her subterfuge up to the curious state of affairs among Nashville's fryers of hot chicken. Such a geographic conceit is expected in a city where, after decades of dominance by Prince's Hot Chicken Shack, four challengers to the throne have emerged. They each tout their recipe as the one, true hot chicken.

I know, thanks to my recent trip, that Buffalo, New York, is a self-aware citadel of fried chicken cookery. But central and west-central Tennessee, home to the metropolis of Nashville and the village of Mason, appear to be places where distinct styles of fried chicken have developed, but, until very recently, no one made proclamations of greatness.

This reclusive nature may have its roots in a kind of shame engendered by Nashville's fried chicken boom and bust of the 1960s. Or perhaps it's because the story of Buffalo chicken wings is fairly tidy, well suited to the twenty-word blurb, while the tale of hot fried chicken as cooked in Tennessee is a messy one, spanning race, class, and 170 miles of roadway.

Over the course of the past five years, the media has made up for lost time. Gus's World Famous Fried Chicken in Mason has become a site of pilgrimage for in-the-know eaters. I may have ferried half of them there. I drove to Mason with Ed Levine, a New York–based writer who wrote a paean to Gus's chicken in *GQ.* I made the trek with Jeffrey Steingarten, who recounted the saga in *Vogue,* but chose to leave out the part about how we arrived two minutes after closing, and I, embarrassed by my failure as a guide, began begging and wheedling and bribing in a successful effort to cadge a cold order of hot chicken that had been previously committed to another customer.

Both Ed and Jeffrey wrote compelling pieces on the joys of eating Gus's spicy fried chicken. But I've come to believe that Gus's might be better appreciated as a vestige of a day when hot fried chicken was not an anomaly but a constant. It was once valued by working-class Southerners in the same way that a pepper-spiked bowl of Saturday-morning menudo is still prized by working-class Americans of Mexican ancestry. Both are basic sustenance that filled the belly, cleared the head, stymied a hangover.

While I am not immune to the charms of Gus's, Nashville is the only American city where an appreciation for hot fried chicken can reach fullest flower. In NashVegas, no one questions the difference between Buffalo heat and Tennessee fire. Here, devotees take pride in the fact that, while Buffalo wings owe their piquancy to a toss in sauce, the fire in local chicken comes at you from any number of sources, including one or more of the following: a dose of cayenne in the frying oil, a splash of Tabasco in the batter, a dash of powdered habanero in the breading, a sprinkle of any ol' dried and powdered pepper atop the finished bird, even a sluice of pepper-infused oil on the pickles that crown that same bird. In Nashville, at least among the drinking class, folks appreciate the kind of heat that compels you to grab a first-aid manual, thumbing wildly for a passage that differentiates between second- and third-degree burns.

O n the drive home from another research trip, I recently stopped off in Nashville for a refresher course in hot chicken. Joe's Hotttt Chicken, a newly opened, six-seat take-away in the suburb of Madison, mixes the most aromatic seasoning blend, shot through with cayenne but also benefiting from what tastes like smoked paprika. Bolton's Hot and Spicy Chicken and Fish in East Nashville was conceived as a tribute to Colombo's, the fabled chicken shack that Bolton Polk once operated at the foot of the Shelby Street Bridge. But the birds that exit their fryers are dry, and the heat of their chicken is somehow muted by a duskiness that bespeaks cayenne long past its prime.

Hotchickens.com, a gingham-trimmed fast-food outlet that opened in 2001, reflects the peculiar Nashville geek-in-a-cowboy-hat zeitgeist by way of its name and its ownership by country music darlings Lorrie Morgan and Sammy Kershaw. As for the chicken, rumored to be spiced and fried according to a recipe similar to Prince's, it's worthy of your patronage if not your devotion.

Speaking of devotion, Prince's Hot Chicken Shack still wins mine, for their four-in-the-morning weekend closing times; for their devotion to gargantuan iron skillets from which emerge some of the crispest, savoriest chicken around; for the architectural precision with which they stack a quarter-chicken atop two slices of white bread, crowning the whole affair with a couple or three pickle slices; and for their heavy hand with the pepper wand, their tendency to swab a thigh with enough hot stuff to prod a drunken patron into a stunned semblance of sobriety.

despite my love of the birds fried by Andre Prince and crew, I am drawn, inextricably, back to Mr. Boo's. Sure, the chicken is good: Diana Bouglea makes every effort to serve hand-cut birds that are less than a day away from the feedlot. Her breasts, which usually weigh in at over a pound, are a tad dry, but rarely have I tasted a breast that meets my standards of juiciness. Diana claims to employ four seasoning steps: First she injects the chicken with liquefied Bouglea peppers. Then she marinates it in Bouglea. Of course, she seasons her flour with Bouglea. And, after deep-frying her bird, she shakes a little extra Bouglea on for good measure. How much she shakes, and whether the particular ground Bouglea she employs is harvested from the leaves, stems, fruits, or rhizomes, determines whether you are eating mild, medium, hot, or what the menu advertises as "The Big Bang!"

I am also drawn to Diana Bouglea herself. I admire her white tennis shoes, which, thanks to a pall of pepper dust, seem to be shading toward claret. And, despite myself, I believe at least half of what the fifty-something-year-old tells me. As we talk, Diana refers again and again to her family's domain, "way down there in Poteet Parish." But it takes me a good hour to extract from her that it is her husband, Mr. Boo, who hails from Louisiana. She, on the other hand, is a local girl, reared on the fiery goodness of Prince's Hot Chicken Shack.

She talks and I play along, asking her to tell me about life down in Cajun Country. She does not skip a beat. "In the early 1900s, about three generations back," she tells me, "the Bouglea family discovered an odd-looking plant growing abroad their farm land in Louisiana, along the Mississippi Delta." I smile, and between bites of chicken, plot a map that places Poteet Parish just this side of the Shelby Street Bridge.

Tennessee Fire
Fried Chicken

MASON, TENNESSEE, AND
MANHATTAN, NEW YORK

More than likely, the Tennessee tradition of fiery chicken pre-
cedes the invention of Buffalo wings by a generation or two. I
would like to tell you that what follows is the first publication
of the recipe made famous by Gus's of Mason, Tennessee. But
that would be a lie. What follows is a slight adaptation of a
recipe created by Michael Romano of Union Square Café for
Blue Smoke in Manhattan. He loves Gus's chicken as much
as I do, and devoted a few days to creating Gus's homage to
it. Michael was gracious to share his recipe; all I did was in-
crease the amount of hot sauce to meet the expectations of
those who have had the pleasure of eating at Gus's.

- 3 small chickens, 3 to 3½ pounds each
- Vegetable or peanut oil for frying
- ½ gallon milk
- ½ cup Texas Pete hot sauce
- ¾ cup kosher salt
- ¼ cup paprika

(*continued*)

- 2 tablespoons cayenne pepper
- ½ cup freshly ground black pepper
- 4 cups all-purpose flour

Pour at least 3 inches of oil into a deep and heavy pot. Heat the oil to 320°. Cut the chickens into 8 pieces each. Remove the wing tips and middle section of the wings. Leave the last section of the wings attached to the breast. Remove the legs and thighs, and separate. Cut the backbone off (you can use for soup). Cut the breast in half down the center of the breastplate, leaving two equal-sized halves with wing sections attached.

Mix the milk in a bowl with the hot sauce and ¼ cup of the kosher salt. Soak the chicken pieces in the seasoned milk marinade for 1 hour. In another bowl, stir the remaining salt, the paprika, and the cayenne and black peppers together with the flour.

Remove the chicken from the milk and dredge in the seasoned flour. Toss the chicken until well coated. Shake off any excess flour from chicken and deep fry, a few pieces at a time, for 12 minutes or more. Remove the breasts from oil when they register 160° and the dark meat when it registers 170°. Drain for two minutes before serving. *Serves 8.*

Carry On, My Wayward Chicken

t he pervasiveness of hot fried chicken is a universal truth, born out by stories of fabled joints like 1960s-era Carrousel Lounge in Macon, Georgia, where old man Hodges sold rotgut liquor and caustically spiced chicken. Phil Walden, the rock-and-roll impresario who boosted the Allman Brothers to superstardom, once told me that Hodges was known for his Wake Up Chicken Special, which registered high enough on the Scoville scale to rouse you from a five-day drunk.

Later, while I was perusing the bins in a used-record store, I discovered that Walden was not the only one who doted on Hodges's hot fried chicken. On a 1972 album, Wet Willie, another of Walden's Capricorn bands, cut an instrumental, entitled "Red Hot Chicken," in tribute to the fire of Hodges's bird.

Follow the musical thread and you expose a deep and abiding reverence for fried chicken spiced to a lip-scalding extreme. More than a quarter-century after Hodges's heyday, the New Jersey–based band Yo La Tengo (critical darlings of the late-'90s independent scene) cut "Hot Chicken #1," "Hot Chicken #2," and "Return to Hot Chicken," in testament to their love of Prince's in Nashville.

I know of no songs cut in tribute to Kansas City fried chicken. If I could play a musical instrument—even if I were able to do nothing more than hum a tune in a key that would not call forth a pack of curs—I would rectify the situation in a moment, for Kansas City is one of the true citadels of poultry cookery. To my mind, K.C.'s worthy of at least a B-side single.

FOURTEEN

The Coronation
of a Kansas City
Roadhouse Queen

like Buffalo, New York—and, for that matter, Nashville, Tennessee—the fried chicken capital of Kansas City owes much of its reputation for excellence to the barroom. Or, more exactly, to the county-line roadhouse set just beyond the reach of local police. I knew this even before I hit the road. Reel off a list of fried chicken spots revered by natives of this sprawling metropolis, and, soon after they cease bemoaning the demise of swankish haunts like the Green Parrot Inn located just north of

Country Club Plaza (America's first planned shopping mall) and the Wishbone (origin point of a certain fabled Italian salad dressing), talk will turn to questions of real import.

Questions like, *Can good chicken be fried in a kitchen not befouled by cigarette smoke, or is carbonized tobacco an essential ingredient?* And, *Is it true that a certain cook of great renown could not face the stove unless she had a tumbler of Seagram's VO at her side?*

New arrivals, untutored in the history of Kansas City chicken cookery, might counter with a few questions of their own like, *Isn't fried chicken supposed to be the province of kindly grandmothers who also darn socks and knit afghans?* And, *Isn't a well-fried chicken an expression of love and family fidelity, not the province of a low-life roadhouse?*

Invariably, the grandmom-and-apple-pie contingent loses out, for, as many a native of Kansas City knows, two roadhouse fry cooks forged the local reputation for fried chicken served with mashed potatoes, cream gravy, green beans, and biscuits. Betty Lucas and Helen Stroud honed their techniques to the tune of clinking beer bottles and a piano player stoked on whiskey and cigarettes.

every cook in town wants a piece of Betty Lucas, the woman Mimi Sheraton once dubbed the "pied piper of chickendom." Known to her admirers as Chicken Betty, she was a peripatetic fryer, a kind of Johnny Appleseed analogue who spread the gospel of pan-fried chicken from roadhouse to restaurant, diner to coffee shop.

Born in 1910 in Nebraska, she grew up on a farm where hundreds of chickens scratched the dirt. "By the time I was thirteen," she once said, "I knew how to catch and kill the chickens, then pluck, clean, and cut them up." In between and sometime concurrent with hitches at various restaurants, Betty worked as a kindergarten teacher and a bookkeeper. But despite health problems that resulted in the eventual installation of a pacemaker, she always returned to the kitchen.

I try to chart her movements over the course of a sixty-plus-year career—and thus the untold cooks who claim to have learned at the elbow of the master—but, while perusing the archives at the local library, I lose count at about fifteen restaurants. One that will linger in my memory was Granny's, where the walls were plastered with photos of real-life grandmothers and a few male patrons dressed in octogenarian drag.

In the end, I face facts: I never knew Chicken Betty. I will never have the opportunity to taste her fried chicken. I will forever pine to have visited her at Boots & Coates, the barroom where she took up the skillet in the early 1970s. I will not eat a midmorning drumstick snack at the Metro Auto Auction's coffee shop, where Calvin Trillin tracked her down in the early 1980s. I will never know the pleasure of snagging a booth at the Westport Diner and biting into a haunch of fried bird while listening to an ancient piano player sing "Roll Out the Barrel."

And so it is that, with a sort of resignation, I take a seat at K.T. Fryers, a suburban fern bar purported to be one of the places where Chicken Betty's recipe—and her spirit—lives on. They get the chicken right: thin of crust and juicy of thigh. And the gravy is a lumpy and cracklin' clogged thing of beauty. But there's no rollicking piano player in sight. Indeed, the only music I hear is a Muzak-tempered ditty made famous by Air Supply, back about the time when Betty would have been bucking and swaying at Boots & Coates. Though a consensus among my best local sources has steered me here, I get the distinct impression that Betty's spirit, in need of a little more action, has taken up residence elsewhere.

Compared with Chicken Betty, Helen Stroud was not so peripatetic. But she was no less lively. Born in 1901 in Wichita, she came to Kansas City as a teenager and worked as an insurance secretary before enrolling in law school and subsequently dropping out to marry a fellow student named Stroud. Somehow—details are murky—this string of events compelled Helen and her beau to open a fireworks stand and then a barbecue restaurant beyond the Kansas City line.

The far-flung location entitled Helen to sell booze on Sunday. And thanks to the booze, Stroud's sometimes drew a boisterous weekend crowd. But Helen never brooked any foolishness. "I was a good bouncer," she told a local reporter in the 1960s. "If a man and a woman didn't come in together, they couldn't dance together."

Over time, the roadhouse's proclaimed specialties of barbecue ribs and sardines gave way to fried chicken. Precious little evidence remains to explain why, save a rumor that, by the late 1940s, chicken was too cheap to ignore. (Surely,

Stroud's motto, "We Choke Our Own Chickens," can't be a relic of the days when Helen killed her own poultry?)

Helen bought fresh chicken, always shipped on ice and never frozen. While Chicken Betty was not immune to the allure of MSG, Helen limited her seasoning to salt and pepper. What's more, she insisted that every bird that exited her kitchen was fried, not in the basket of a deep fryer, but in a pan.

Perhaps she believed in some alchemical effect only achieved when iron, chicken, and flour meet. It's more likely that Helen knew well what I now suspect: that great pan-fried required close attention, while deep-frying is almost set-it-and-forget-it easy. Knowledge of the latter can lead to laziness on the part of a cook and, as a result, chicken unworthy of Helen's good name.

today, pan-fried still means something in Kansas City. It's a talismanic conjunction of words, an incantation of good food recognized by everyone. Here, pan-fried is heralded in the same manner that a suit maker trumpets hand-stitched lapels and functional sleeve buttons. It shouts to the world that someone laid his or her hand on the skillet, that a Seussian machine did not accomplish this work of frying, that these pieces of chicken did not achieve their crunch by means of a conveyor-belt crawl through the oil.

Thanks to the stewardship of the two successive owners that followed Helen Stroud, her namesake restaurant is still revered by locals as a citadel of pan-fried chicken. It helps that

Stroud's looks the part. At the original location, a brown, shingle-lapped wreck in the shadow of the Troost Avenue Viaduct, the windows are clouded by diesel fumes and smudged by generations of grime-stained fingers. Here, the chicken has the right crunch, the mashed potatoes taste of the earth, and the green beans collapse in a heap like they should.

But all that said, the clientele now appears a bit dowdy, a little too family-focused. Sure, Stroud's occasionally rolls out the upright piano on Saturday nights and encourages everyone to sing along, but in the fluorescent light it seems more like a pageant staged for the benefit of people like me, who were not lucky enough to be in attendance when the real shit flew.

For that sense of raffish delight—and chicken that meets the same pan-fried standards as Stroud's—I make my way west of downtown to Opal's, which, despite a cheery paint job and a collection of art that might have been ordered direct from the studios of Bob Timberlake, conjures a vague seediness.

I can't quite put my finger on the source of the funk until, as I drag a thigh through a puddle of gravy, my dining companion, local restaurant critic Charles Ferruzza, tells me a little secret. It seems that before opening a restaurant named for the fry cook's grandmother, the owner of Opal's ran Club Cabaret, a drag bar featuring a coterie of locally famous illusionists.

I ponder this information while resolving that, although Opal's is not my ideal, their chicken is great. Indeed, it may be the closest thing to a twenty-first-century roadhouse where, if Betty and Helen and I wanted to knock back a few shots and talk poultry, we would be welcomed with open arms and cheap drinks.

Skillet-Fried K.C. Yard Bird with Skillet-Lickin' Gravy

KANSAS CITY, MISSOURI

Gravy was once an integral part of most fried chicken recipes. As Margaret Birdwell notes in 1953's Kentucky Fare, *"Cream gravy is fried chicken's almost invariable accompaniment." Somewhere along the way, gravy fell out of favor. One of the remaining strongholds is the Midwest, specifically Missouri and Kansas, where fried chicken without gravy is like a candle without a wick.*

- 1 chicken weighing 3 to 4 pounds (the smaller, the better), cut into 8–10 pieces
- 1 egg
- 2–2½ cups milk

(*continued*)

■ 1 tablespoon salt, plus more to taste

■ 1 tablespoon pepper, plus more to taste

■ 2 teaspoons Accent seasoning

■ Peanut oil into which you mix about
3 tablespoons bacon grease

■ 1 cup all-purpose flour, plus 1 tablespoon
more for gravy

Beat egg and 1 cup of the milk until frothy. Dip chicken pieces individually, shaking off excess and resting on wax-paper-lined tray. Sprinkle both sides of chicken with 1 tablespoon salt and pepper, and Accent. Heat oil in pan, at a depth of about 1½ inches, over medium-high heat. Toss each chicken piece in a paper bag filled with 1 cup flour, and shake off excess as you remove each piece. Beginning with the dark meat, slip chicken into pan, skin-side down, and fry at approximately 300–325° for 5–6 minutes. Turn and fry for 5–6 minutes more. Cover partially and fry for another 15 minutes, turning as needed. Remove when chicken is coppery brown or when an internal thermometer registers 170° for dark meat, 160° for white meat. Drain on a wire rack.

Make gravy by pouring off all but 1 tablespoon of the grease from skillet. Return skillet to stove and place over low burner. Toss in the 1 tablespoon flour and scrape up cracklings and other bits from bottom. Brown flour until it turns the color of a football. Pour in 1–1½ cups milk and stir until smooth. Season to taste with additional salt and pepper. Pour gravy over mashed potatoes, not over chicken. *Serves 4.*

Jail Birds

fried chicken once evoked a rural idyll, a time and place where many cooks had the luxury, the inclination to devote hours on end to the preparation of Sunday supper. But as America has urbanized, so has American cooking. So has fried chicken.

The rural-to-urban migration has been a catalyst for welcoming new fryers to the fold. As we will discover in the chapter that follows, first-generation immigrants have embraced fried chicken as a symbol of assimilation, as well as a means of gaining financial independence. But urban life begets urban travails. Like crime. If a recent perusal of a newspaper morgue is to be believed, fried-chicken-related crime is on the rise. Among the recent highlights:

■ In November of 1993, Fareedullah Nawabi was arrested for selling guns from the drive-thru window of Mama's Fried Chicken in New York City. Upon seizing over sixty pieces of ordnance including an assault rifle and a few machine pistols, Police Commissioner Raymond Kelly observed, "Obviously some deadly side dishes were being served in the Bronx."

■ In September of 2002, Carlos Ayala, an employee of KFC in Mill Valley, California, was arrested for selling marijuana while at work. His arrest was prompted by a drive-thru customer who asked for extra biscuits with his box of fried chicken. Instead of forking over the biscuits, Ayala allegedly handed him two nickel bags of marijuana.

Is there a moral to this story? Nope. Just be wary of the drive-thru clerk who tells you that extra biscuits cost . . . well, extra.

FIFTEEN

Seoul Food

Sam Lee is a businessman who happens to fry chicken. Upon leaving Seoul, South Korea, in 1971, he settled in the Los Angeles suburb of Glendale. After years of menial labor and frugal ways, he saved enough money to buy a liquor store. In 1988 he sold his liquor store and moved north to Seattle, in search of better schools for his children.

Like hordes of other new arrivals, he gravitated to sprawling Pike Place Market, beloved by tourists who photograph the salmon-tossing antics of fishmongers, revered by local gastronomes who prowl the day stalls in search of bok choy and bing cherries. Sam spent a good six weeks at the market, taking note of traffic patterns and customer preferences, in search of a cash business he could buy.

Chicken Valley was on the block. And though Sam knew nothing of its beginnings in the 1920s, he liked what he saw: low overhead, a steady stream of customers, a regular exchange of fives and ones. At the time Sam bought Chicken Valley it was known as a retailer of fresh poultry—quail, pheasant, chicken, duck, goose, turkey—and, to a lesser extent, as a vendor of fried chicken. When Sam bought the counter-based business, he changed that balance, introducing fried rice and devoting less space to the display of dressed poultry. "I follow the trends," Sam tells me by way of explanation. "I serve what my customers want."

As we talk, our feet hiked on opposite sides of an alley dumpster, Sam resists, and then finally succumbs to my questions about what it means to be a Korean man frying chicken in the States. "I fry American-style chicken," he tells me. "I tried to serve Korean spices, but that is dangerous for a businessman in America. I can't serve kim chee; that would confuse my customers. They see my face and know I am Asian, but they taste my fried chicken and know it's American. That's what stays with them. But I still try small things: When I added fried rice, I decided to use Korean-style, Japanese-style sticky rice."

Sam's musings about the danger of serving Asian-spiced

chicken call to my mind the typical immigrant's passion for assimilation. Though now on the decline among newer generations, this push to become American at all costs owed some of its origins to fear of social and economic ostracism of the sort that gave birth to the Japanese internment camps of the 1940s. For people like Sam, such fear manifests itself in the nagging knowledge that if one is to thrive here, he must play by American rules.

S am Lee's Chicken Valley does not claim to be a fulcrum of fried chicken cookery. And despite what Oprah Winfrey and legions of her fans pledge, crosstown favorite Ezell's Fried Chicken is not poised to be the next citadel of fried fowl. But there exists now in Seattle, and dozens of other American cities, the possibility of a new style of cuisine that shuns geographic labels and ethnic imperatives in favor of cultural complement. That possibility got me on a plane, bound for Seattle. I know there are pitfalls aplenty, among them a tendency toward strumpeted fusion, but in opening the door to possibility, a city like Seattle entertains the possibility of great new tastes.

Over the course of my travels, I've seen this possibility manifest at a model train shop in Eureka Springs, Arkansas, where a man of Indian descent sells homemade samosas and freezer-case pastries amid displays of HO-gauge rail cars and cabooses. I've seen this reality in practice at a donut-teriyaki stand in San Francisco, California, where, after a couple years of selling General Tsao chicken from a steam table and maple long johns from an adjacent pastry case, dim sum carts laden with maple-glazed buns now make noontime rounds. But I've never been more aware of the possibilities than I was on a recent trip to Atlanta, Georgia.

I f Sam Lee *were* to incorporate Korean spices and techniques, his chicken might taste a lot like the birds fried at Harue, a hipster coffee shop set in a former Wendy's on Buford Highway, Atlanta's multiethnic main street. On the day I dine, I am the sole white face in the crowd. I bet I am also the oldest.

The interior is a cipher: Hangdog adolescents outfitted in Hello Kitty couture slouch in birch wood chairs affixed with tieback pastel slipcovers. Club music blares from overhead speakers, giving me the impression that, in less than ten minutes, the floor might be cleared to make way for an afternoon rave.

When I make an attempt to chat up a teenage girl sitting in the corner, drinking bubble tea, she offers this much information before growing bored: Harue is a Korean version of a Japanese *kissaten,* which, if I understand her correctly, is an Eastern take on a Western coffee shop. That means, I tell her, the food of Harue has its origins in American coffee shop fare, first interpreted to suit the tastes of Japanese in Japan, and then reinterpreted to suit the tastes of Koreans now living in America. "Yes, you have it," she says. "They serve Japanese-Korean-American food. Try the fried chicken."

I do. It's hacked into irregular pieces, dusted in corn-starch, and fried to a crunch. It's very good. Preceding each platter of fried chicken come a half-dozen saucers of pickled vegetables, including kimchee. Alongside the chicken, wait-resses deposit saucers of sesame-salt-pepper mix as well as a sweetish hot sauce, more than likely Sriracha, a Vietnamese brand.

The table is set with a choice of chopsticks and forks. I reach for the less familiar conveyance. And after fumbling a wing and then a quarter-thigh, I dip a nugget of breast meat attached to wishbone, first into the Sriracha, then into the sesame mix, and finally into my mouth. I chew around the wishbone, savoring the vaguely sweet taste of the meat, the heat of pepper, the muskiness of the sesame. Before I can get my chopsticks around the next bite, my waitress returns, bearing a platter of shredded cabbage. It's topped with a vaguely pink dressing that she seems loath to explain. "It's special," she says. "It's special." One bite of the slaw and sauce and I know what she means. It's akin to the "special sauce" on a McDon-ald's Big Mac.

I turn to seek confirmation from Miss Bubble Tea, but she has departed. After a couple more failed chopstick attempts, I pick up a fork and dive into my meal. As I eat, I think of Sam Lee, wishing that he were by my side, that he could pick up a fork and taste the future of American fried chicken.

Korean-American Fried Chicken

SEATTLE, WASHINGTON
(WITH A TASTE OF ATLANTA, GEORGIA)

*Korean fried chicken is a dish of assimilation. In my travels,
I have encountered many a Korean who, in an effort to cook
American, has forgone his native palate in favor of a per-
ceived North American standard. Among the pleasant ex-
ceptions has been Chicken Valley, where, despite Sam Lee's
claims, I taste something of his native Seoul in the crisp skin.
Even more pronounced is the chicken fried at Harue.*

- 1 chicken weighing 3 to 4 pounds (the smaller, the better), cut into 8–10 pieces
- ¼ cup soy sauce
- ¾ cup rice wine vinegar (the seasoned kind)
- ¼ cup cornstarch
- ½ cup all-purpose flour
- 1 tablespoon salt
- Peanut oil
- 1 cup sesame seeds, toasted
- 1 cup sea salt

- 1 cup black pepper
- 1 cup Sriracha hot chili sauce

Combine soy sauce and vinegar in a large bowl. Add chicken, and marinate for 2 hours, turning occasionally. Combine cornstarch, flour, and salt in a paper bag. Add chicken, shaking until very lightly coated. Remove to a wire rack, shaking again to loosen any stray flour.

Heat 3 inches of oil to 350° in a deep and heavy pot. Fry at 325° for 12–15 minutes until chicken is blond-brown with russet highlights, or until an internal thermometer registers 170° for dark meat, 160° for white meat. Place chicken on wire rack to drain.

Portion sesame seeds, sea salt, and pepper into fourths and place mix of each into four small bowls, one for each guest. Portion hot sauce in same manner, into 4 more bowls. Dip chicken alternately into sesame-salt-pepper mix and/or hot sauce. *Serves 4.*

Lard Almighty

Lard. Many trees have been felled, much ink spilled in condemning this blunt noun. When the great baseball player Satchel Paige advised, "Avoid fried meats which angry up the blood," chances are he was talking about meats fried in lard.

But lard is a hard habit to shake. Writing in 1860 of the South's devotion to all things fried and of the preferred medium for frying, Dr. John S. Wilson of Columbus, Georgia, observed, "Hog's lard is the very oil that moves the machinery of life, and they would just as soon think of dispensing with tea, coffee, or tobacco . . . as with the essence of hog." One supposes that the good and temperate Dr. Wilson lamented his fellow man's love of lard.

Of late the dietary pendulum has swung in favor of pig fat. Turns out that it's lower in saturated fat than butter. A whole new generation of cooks is learning to love the crispness of a drumstick fried in the good stuff. Scott Peacock, whose story follows, is one of those converts.

But like dolphin fish reborn as mahi-mahi, lard may not survive this resurgence with its name intact. Niman Ranch, the specialty meat provider, is now marketing decidedly American lard by way of a decidedly French name, *saindoux.*

SIXTEEN

A Sonnet in Two Birds

Scott Peacock, chef of Watershed, a hip, celadon-hued restaurant and wine bar in Decatur, Georgia, fries chicken on Tuesdays. And only on Tuesdays. John Fleer, chef of the Inn at Blackberry Farm, a luxe resort in the Great Smoky Mountains of northeastern Tennessee, fries chicken on Saturdays. And only on Saturdays.

In the modern South—where fried chicken is oftentimes a dish of immediate resort, a fast-food commodity purchased by the box and on

the go—once-a-week restaurant chicken feeds are both romantic and practical. Romantic in that they bespeak a time
when fried chicken was known among many rural folk as a
farm-raised, Sunday indulgence, a gospel bird. Practical in that
the two-plus days of prep work now employed by these chefs
is onerous.

Prevailing wisdom—as communicated by Southern cook-
books of the past century, especially by those books geared
toward home cooks—leads you to believe that fried chicken
is among the most elemental of dishes. Many contemporary
recipes dictate such simplicity that, if the fried chicken actually tastes as good as promised, I'm inclined to look to sorcery
as the reason.

Cut and wash the chicken, dredge in flour, season with
salt, and fry. That's what Mary Randolph, author of the 1824
masterwork *The Virginia Housewife,* would have you do. And if
you talk to a Southerner with puritanical culinary inclinations, they are likely to subscribe to the Randolphian school.
These cooks believe in paying homage to great ingredients by
allowing their integrity to shine through.

But chicken ain't what it used to be. Big-breasted, spindly-
legged birds, raised in close confinement and shot through
with all manner of growth-promoting hormones and anti-
biotics, are now the rule. Yard birds raised *en plein air,* scratching about for scraps and grain while developing stronger
muscles and, by extension, darker and more flavorful meat, are
the exception. And so it follows that, if chicken ain't what it
used to be, then neither is fried chicken.

One of the abiding themes of my pilgrimage has proven to be that, throughout the country, the most intriguing fried chicken dishes seem to be served by restaurants where the cooks monkey the most with the birds. In the South, this trend rings truest. At Gus's, chicken marinates in a viscous, pepper-laced solution that resembles crimson yogurt and gives the chicken a lip-tingling heat; Austin Leslie swears by topping his deep-fried chicken with a confetti of garlic and parsley as well as a spot of pickle juice; and at Greenwood's the chicken emerges a bit dry from the fryer, but is redeemed by dipping the breasts in pepper vinegar and then drizzling them with honey.

And yet, these folks have nothing on Peacock and Fleer, the aforementioned weekly fryers. I am not inclined to posit that either cooks the best fried chicken in the South—or even that such a such a designation has merit—but I am convinced that both gentlemen have achieved a modern mastery, balancing age-old ways and new imperatives of flavor.

Scott Peacock's chicken *looks* simple. The presentation is straightforward. Breast, leg, and thigh, each piled one atop the other on a white plate, each burnished a coppery brown. Accompaniments are whipped potatoes and garlicky green beans. Fat and fluffy biscuits too.

I bite into the breast. The crust has fused with the skin,

and it crackles upon contact with my teeth. You can actually *hear* the crunch. And while most white meat is dry, woody even, this bird squirts juice. Not grease, but juice, rivulets of pork-scented chicken broth. After spending a few hours at Watershed, talking chicken with Peacock, scribbling notes as he advanced various theories of cookery that both met and confounded my expectations, I was prepared to be disappointed.

No taste could be worth brining the bird for twenty-four hours in a saltwater solution, soaking it for an additional day in buttermilk, and then, after rolling the salted and peppered pieces in a mix of flour and a smidgen of cornstarch, frying them in a fifty-fifty mix of butter and lard infused with country ham. But there it is, on the plate, for all to admire: the perfect fried chicken breast.

It did not surprise me to hear Peacock say that he prefers to fry his chicken in a skillet. "Skillet cooking works from the bottom to the bone," he told me. "It's slower, more seductive than deep frying, like taking a warm bath instead of a scalding dip." And yet, although he dearly loved his grandmother, Peacock is not the kind of cook who wields her old skillet.

Instead, he fries his chicken in an oversized Italian-made stainless-steel pan that will accommodate twenty pieces. And then there's the matter of frying medium. Though he grew up in southern Alabama where the soil is a sandy loam, perfect for growing peanuts, he came to see that the peanut oil with which he was accustomed to cooking couldn't match the flavor punch of the aforementioned lard and butter admixture favored by his eighty-something-year-old mentor, Edna Lewis of Freetown, Virginia.

If forced to categorize his ethic, I would label Peacock a neo-traditionalist. His career has taken him from cooking quail at a hunt camp in southern Georgia, to serving broiled lobsters alongside a nasturtium salad at the Georgia governor's mansion. Along the way, Peacock has honed a very personal cuisine. Granted, he'd be the first to pay his due to his longtime friend and present housemate, Lewis, revered as a grande dame of the South. But by the sheer act of frying chicken this well, Peacock lays claim to his own place in the pantheon.

John Fleer's sweet-tea-marinated fried chicken will be cold by the time you taste it. Well, maybe it won't actually be cold—room temperature might be the best way to describe it. No matter, it won't be fresh from the fryer, for it was cooked about seven in the morning. More than likely, you will bite into your first drumstick on one of the switchback trails that wend around Hurricane Mountain, eventually leading back to the Inn at Blackberry Farm. That's where, since 1992, Fleer has been cooking in a style that he's dubbed Foothills Cuisine.

Fleer came up with the idea of tea-brining while conferring with his sous-chef: "We were talking about how brines incorporate salt and liquid and acid, discussing how a little red wine never hurt. And then it hit me: sweet tea, the house wine of the South. . . . It's always seemed like the hardest part of my job has been packing five-star expectations into the green boxes we hand out for picnic lunches. I had been searching for something that was definitively Southern and distinctly ours. That was it."

On Wednesday, Fleer and his crew make tea. Sweet tea with lemon, the same brew served in hundreds of lunchrooms across the South. After stirring salt in to make a brine, the cooks submerge the chicken—they use legs and thighs only—in the marinade. Two days in the refrigerator follow, during which the salt carries the musky sweetness of the tea throughout the chicken. Early each Saturday the morning crew drain the birds before soaking them in a buttermilk and egg solution and then, finally, rolling the chicken twice in a mixture of cornflour and wheat flour spiked with salt and pepper and Old Bay seasoning.

I am present one recent Saturday morning when the first batch emerges from the fryer. The crust boasts a kind of pleasantly gritty exterior. But while Peacock's fused with the skin, Fleer's crust announces autonomy. As for the meat itself, the brine gives the legs and thighs a muted herbaceous quality that, if I were not aware of its source, I might attribute to unlikely origins, say bourbon or bitters or prune juice.

But Fleer's chicken, served hot from the fryer, is disappointing. Thanks to the heavy jacket developed during the double battering, that autonomous crust proves not to be an asset but a liability. It's tough. Truth be told, I don't realize the genius of what Fleer and his crew are up to until later that

same day. I am an hour down the highway, when I start digging through the box that, upon checking out, I found waiting on my passenger seat.

Most guests get their first taste of Fleer's chicken the way
he intends them to—after forging a stream or ascending a
mountain. I, on the other hand, have merely set the cruise
control and pushed aside a cob of basil-marinated corn, a tub
of creamy pineapple coleslaw, a sesame cheddar biscuit, a
deviled egg, and a marshmallow-smeared oatmeal cookie
sandwich, before finding my prize: a cardboard box-within-a-
box of the type that Chinese takeout restaurants favor.

Within are a leg and a thigh. In the six hours out of the
fryer, they've mellowed. What's more, the sweet tea flavor has
come to the fore. The crust that was unyielding at seven in
the morning has softened to a point still shy of collapse. Now
pliable, now a kind of cornmeal-cracklin' appetizer wrapped
around a drumstick, it proves to be the ideal vessel for the
odd but delicious consommé of chicken and Lipton's that
dribbles down my chin.

ven after eating my fill of the fried chicken cooked by
Peacock and Fleer, I remain unsure about what con-
clusions I should draw from their approaches. Both are ardent students of Southern cookery. Both are committed to
working with fresh, local ingredients. Both have a predilection for buttermilk and a resolve that chicken—and for that
matter, most any domesticated pork or poultry—tastes best

when brined. But are these guys technocrats, intent upon reinventing fried chicken? Or are they fellow travelers in the tradition, bent upon wresting the most flavor and succulence from a bird that can be, at times, uncooperative?

Beats me, but their chicken eats great. And neither chef is secretive about sharing recipes. If you want to try to replicate Peacock's, just pick up a copy of his book *The Gift of Southern Cooking,* coauthored with Lewis. It's right there on page 104. As for Fleer, he's also at work on a book. And you can bet that when he hits the cooking school circuit, sweet-tea-brined fried chicken—served cold—will send his students into a collective swoon. Until that fine day, an adaptation of his recipe follows.

Sweet-Tea Fried Chicken

WALLAND, TENNESSEE

John Fleer is a thinking man's chef, a onetime doctoral candidate in religion who chucked it all for a career in the kitchen. One of the best ideas to spring from his mind is this brined chicken, which manages to pay tribute to the tradi-

tional South of days past and the multicultural South still on the horizon.

- 8 chicken leg quarters, cut into thighs and drumsticks
- 1 quart brewed tea, double strength
- 1 lemon, quartered
- 1 cup sugar
- ½ cup kosher salt
- 1 quart ice water
- 3 cups all-purpose flour
- 2 cups cornflour (or fish fry)
- 2 tablespoons Old Bay seasoning
- 1 tablespoon chili powder
- 1 teaspoon salt
- 1 teaspoon pepper
- 8 eggs
- 1 cup buttermilk
- Peanut oil

Combine tea, lemon, sugar, and kosher salt, and simmer for 5 minutes or until salt and sugar are completely dissolved. Pour in ice water and cool brine completely. Submerge thighs and drumsticks in brine for 48 hours.

(continued)

Remove to a wire rack and allow chicken to drain. Combine 2 cups of the flour and the cornflour, Old Bay, chili powder, salt, and pepper in a large bowl. Place remaining 1 cup flour in a medium bowl, and in a third bowl beat eggs with buttermilk. Line up bowls of flour, egg-buttermilk mixture, and flour-cornflour mixture, in that order. Coat the chicken in the flour, then the egg-buttermilk mixture, and then the flour-cornflour mixture, applying pressure to ensure even adherence. Let the chicken sit in the refrigerator for ½ hour before frying.

Pour oil into a heavy pot at a depth of at least 3 inches. Heat oil to 300°. Fry chicken, submerged in oil, for 15 minutes, or until an internal thermometer registers 170° for dark meat, 160° for white meat. Drain on a rack. Cool to room temperature, and then place in refrigerator for at least 4 hours and no more than 24. Serve cool from a picnic basket or cold, straight from the fridge. *Serves 8.*

SEVENTEEN

A Chicken Coda

tales of excellence in fowl fried by Southerners bring us back, of course, to Jim Villas. "To know about fried chicken," he wrote, "you have to have been weaned and reared on it in the South. Period."

Remember how I railed against his provincial bluster? Our last two cooks, Peacock and Fleer, may well prove Villas right. But I doubt it. Though I can't imagine coming across two non-Southern chefs who lavish as much attention upon the frying of chicken as they do, I am now more convinced than ever that there's a Yankee—or maybe a Korean man or a Serbian woman—out there right now, brining birds, rendering lard, doing his or her damnedest to prove Villas wrong.

Indeed, ethnicity may well be the defining characteristic of modern American fried chicken. In days past, stereotypes held that kerchiefed women of African descent were wizards of the skillet. To many Americans they were kitchen chattel, imbued with an innate ability to fry poultry that emerged from the kitchen devoid of grease and, perhaps more importantly, absent any claim to provenance. (Of course, many a white woman knew her way around a stove; but, at least for the moment, I am thinking of prevailing public perception, of how we Americans were wont to tell the story of fried chicken.)

In the intervening 200 years, much has changed. And much stays the same. Nowadays, the belief that fried chicken is an inscrutable product of culinary legerdemain is in decline. What's more, we now recognize that those African American women and men—most of whom either lived in the South or were one generation removed from Dixie—had family names as well as given names. With a little luck and the passing of a few more generations, they may yet garner the respect they deserve.

Meanwhile, here we are in twenty-first-century America. The Census Bureau tells us that our nation is now truly multiethnic. And so do my travels. If my read is right, a new generation of immigrants is claiming the mantle once consigned to Americans of African descent. And a new generation of fry cooks is now working at the fringes of society, reinterpreting our beloved fried chicken. Historian Karen Hess once explained this process of incremental change in the American diet by way of a Chinese expression that might be translated as *wok presence*. The idea is that each cook arrives at the stove with his or her own palate, his or her own cultural inclinations, and no matter how closely that cook might follow an established recipe, they are predisposed to refashion a dish to reflect, at least in part, their own traditions. And so it is with chicken as fried in my America.

I began my research propelled by the belief that fried chicken transcended the provincial, and, in the stories of immigrants, I found just what I sought. That's not to say I was closed to new ideas, for I also discovered much that surprised me. Conventional wisdom holds that the best fried chicken is cooked in American homes, in kitchens where cast iron skillets are passed down from one generation to the next like a kind of carbonized dowry. Until I hit the road, it's a belief to which I too ascribed. But two generations of American entrepreneurs and cooks have worked—in unsuspecting concert—to reinvent fried chicken. Indeed, my pilgrimage has led me to believe that the most compelling fried chicken stories of today are tales of commerce.

Over the past two or three generations, we have adapted a farmwoman's dish to suit our consumer culture. We have applied the faster-cheaper-better mantra to all facets of the fried chicken experience. In short, by commodifying fried chicken, we have made it more distinctly American. By means of factory farming, we drove down the price of poultry to the point where nearly everyone can afford it. We invented pressure-fryers and micronic oil filters for our restaurants. And, in time, we overlaid the archetypal family meal—fried chicken, mashed potatoes, green beans, and biscuits—with the efficiencies and imperatives of fast food, creating a new perspective on what it means to eat American.

Some might choose to see these changes as deleterious, and I see their point. But I do not subscribe to such doomsaying. I'm inclined to take the bad with the good. I believe that the commodification of fried chicken bespeaks the process by which this dish has become iconic in the first place. It's the same process by which entrepreneurial ethnic cooks of today make fried chicken their own, the process by which chefs with roving palates are refashioning fried chicken to fit an America of which we have gleaned but a taste.

Appendix

Pecking Orders:
Thoughts on Technique,
Ingredients, Equipment
& My Little Black Book of
Chicken Houses

This book offers two different ways to get your fried chicken fix. If you're keen on making your own, read on for a few tips on technique. Or, if you'd rather gas up the car and go barreling across America in search of a great fried bird, skip to page 175, where I offer a roster of chicken houses I believe to be worthy of pilgrimage.

Thoughts on Technique

Chicken is among the most modified of dishes. By modified, I mean that when referring to chicken, especially to *fried* chicken, we frequently attach an adjective or adverb—a modifier. Modifiers of yore were likely to vouch for the quality of the underlying bird, as in *yellow-leg fried chicken,* a reference to well-fed birds girded with a layer of yellowish chicken fat. Time of harvest was once important. Think of *spring chicken,* a reference to the days before commercial henhouses, when, though hens might lay eggs year-round, they were inclined to sit on eggs only during the warm-weather months. Six weeks after hatching, a spring pullet held the promise of tender fried chicken.

In the modern recipes I showcase, most of the modifiers have their origins in people and places, in the marinades and spice mixes that are traditional to their cookery. In many cases, these recipes are my interpretations of the dishes I ate while on the road. Others come straight from the cook in question.

When pondering a recipe, don't pay attention to defenders of the fried chicken canon who proclaim there is one true method, handed down from on high by the alpha fry cook. That's a load of hooey. Any good cook will take issue with some technique I advance, will want to tweak the recipes that follow, will work to make them his or her own. That said, here are a few guiding principles to keep in mind when you heft your skillet to the stovetop.

Thoughts on Ingredients

When possible, I use anything but regular-ol' grocery store birds. Call them free-range chickens. Call them pastured poultry. Call them air-dried fryers. In most cases, they taste better, are butchered better, are a far better buy (even at a two- or threefold premium) than the cheap stuff. Oh, and unless otherwise specified, any of these recipes will taste better if you brine the chicken for as little as four hours and as much as twenty-four in a gallon of water into which you dissolve a cup of salt.

I usually prefer chickens cut into the dual breast, wing,

thigh, drumstick portions now standard in most grocery stores. But for any bird that tips the scales at more than three pounds, I cut the breasts crosswise into two portions, for a total of ten pieces. If you want to buy whole chickens and cut them up yourself, you might want to invest in a tome like *The Complete Book of Chicken*, written by the editors of *Cook's Illustrated* magazine. Though they snub fried chicken, devoting just twelve of the 486 pages to our beloved subject, they do provide a clear and well-illustrated primer on butchering poultry. If you cook your way through this book and are still looking for more fried chicken recipes, try Damon Lee Fowler's *Fried Chicken: The World's Best Recipes from Memphis to Milan, from Buffalo to Bangkok*. If you fall in love with frying and want to move beyond chicken, try John Martin Taylor's definitive *Fearless Frying*.

If lard is specified in the recipe, get fresh leaf lard from your butcher. But if all you can find is the shelf-stable hydrogenated stuff, you might as well go with Crisco (or a similar vegetable shortening), supplemented by a bit of bacon grease. If you choose oil, make it peanut oil, which has a better flavor and a higher smoke point than many others. A little bacon grease won't hurt here either.

Thoughts on Equipment

At a bare minimum, have on hand a cast-iron or other heavy skillet of at least ten inches in diameter and two inches in depth. Get a wider one if you can, for that means more chicken per skillet and less batch cooking. If you are buying a new skillet, choose a model with a lid. Lodge Manufacturing of South Pittsburgh, Tennessee, makes a wide variety of cast-iron models that are available at your local hardware store or at www.lodgemfg.com. Some of these recipes call for deep-frying. To do that you need a heavy skillet or pot at least four inches deep. You will also benefit from a candy/oil thermometer with a clip to fix on the side of the pot and an instant-read thermometer to measure the doneness of chicken pieces. If you lack such vessels and thermometers, you can modify oil amounts and cooking times, bringing them into line with the basic skillet-fried recipe on page 93.

Last, keep in mind that most of these recipes are easily doubled. But if you plan on serving a crowd, be sure to check the seasoning; that's the first thing to go out of whack when it comes to fried chicken.

My Little Black Book
of Favorite Chicken Houses

Keep in mind that many of these spots are small, family-owned enterprises. As such they may not be open for business seven days a week. (Some owners and staff work eight days a week.) In any event, call ahead to be sure they're open when you plan to visit. And always be respectful of local eaters. Remember, they were there first.

NORTHEAST

Anchor Bar
1047 Main St., Buffalo,
    New York
716-886-8920

Beppe
45 E. 22nd St., New York,
    New York
212-982-8422

Blue Smoke
116 E. 27th St., New York,
    New York
212-447-7733

Chalfonte Hotel
309 Howard St., Cape May,
    New Jersey
609-898-1265

New Caporal
3772 Broadway, New York,
    New York
212-862-8986

Sal's Birdland
1851 Stone Rd., Rochester,
    New York
585-621-1040

SOUTH

Breakfast Klub
3711 Travis St., Houston,
    Texas
713-528-8561

Frenchy's
3919 Scott St., Houston, Texas
713-748-2233

Greenwood's on Green Street
1087 Green St., Roswell,
    Georgia
770-992-5383

Gus's World Famous
    Fried Chicken
505 Hwy. 70 W., Mason,
    Tennessee
901-294-2028

Harue Café
872 Buford Hwy., Atlanta,
    Georgia
770-220-3013

Inn at Blackberry Farm
1471 West Miller's Cove Rd.,
    Walland, Tennessee
865-984-8166

Jacques-Imo's
8324 Oak St.,
New Orleans,
Louisiana
504-861-0886

Julep Restaurant
1305 E. Northside Dr.,
Jackson, Mississippi
601-982-5107

Mr. Boo's
501 Donelson Pike,
Nashville,
Tennessee
615-391-9300

Prince's Hot Chicken
Shack
123 Ewing Dr.,
Nashville,
Tennessee
615-226-9442

Son's Place
160 Hurt St., Atlanta,
Georgia
404-581-0530

Watershed
406 W. Ponce de Leon Ave.,
Decatur, Georgia
404-378-4900

Whole Truth Church and
Lunchroom
515 Walnut St. S., Wilson,
North Carolina
252-237-5595

Willie Mae's Scotch House
2401 St. Anne St.,
New Orleans,
Louisiana
504-822-9503

MIDWEST

Belgrade Gardens
401 E. State St., Barberton,
Ohio
330-745-0113

Eat N Run
8040 S. Ashland Ave.,
Chicago, Illinois
773-892-0867

Gourmet Fried Chicken
43 E. Cermak, Chicago,
   Illinois
312-326-3450

Harold's Chicken Shack
Multiple locations throughout Chicago, Illinois
773-723-9006

Milich's Village Inn
4444 Cleveland Massillon Rd.,
   Barberton, Ohio
330-825-4553

Opal's Kitchen
423 Southwest Blvd., Kansas
   City, Missouri
816-472-6725

St. Paul's Church Picnic
   (Second Sunday in August)
New Alsace, Indiana
812-623-2631

Stroud's
1015 E. 85th St., Kansas City,
   Missouri
816-333-2132

WEST

Chicken Valley
1507 Pike Pl., Seattle,
   Washington
206-624-2774

Ezell's
502 23rd Ave., Seattle,
   Washington
206-324-2121

Pollo Campero
Multiple locations in Los
   Angeles, California (and
   elsewhere)
323-587-3743

Roscoe's Chicken and
   Waffles
1518 N. Gower St.,
   Los Angeles, California
323-466-7453

Zeke's Smokehouse
2209 Honolulu Ave.,
   Montrose (Los Angeles),
   California
818-957-7045

Thanks

My deep appreciation goes to recipe testers Lenore Hobbs, Beckett Howorth, and Sharon Hunt of Oxford, and to the Writers' Colony at Dairy Hollow for a fellowship that afforded me a month of work in their culinary suite. (If you are in need of a quiet place to write and cook, get thee to their nunnery.) Different versions of a couple of these essays originally appeared in *Gourmet* and *Attaché*. I thank my editors there, Jane Daniels Lear, Lance Elko, and Cari Jackson, for unflagging support.

My wife, Blair Hobbs, ate fried chicken with gusto and read the manuscript with a gimlet eye and a knowing palate. My friend and colleague Linda Peal offered strong edits and insights for which I am thankful. My pal Amy Evans shot the fine photographs that adorn these pages. Without the energy and intellect of my agent, David Black, this book would never have been born. I also sing the praises of my editor, Jennifer Hershey, a kind woman with a sharp pencil and a keen eye for improving a manuscript. Her assistant, Rich Florest, was a prince.

Many of the people who took me in, fed me meals, shared their secrets, lent me cars, and listened to me babble on and on about fried chicken are chronicled in the text. Among those who are not, and to whom I am indebted, are Hsiao-Ching Chou, Peter McKee, Susan Tucker, Tyler Florence, Ron Brandon, Paige Osborne, Jessica Harris, John Martin Taylor,

Becky Mercuri, Tom Franklin, Beth Ann Fennelly, Marc Smirnoff, Lolis Elie, John Egerton, Ronni Lundy, Elizabeth Sims, Robin Kline, Sarah Etheridge, Sara Roahen, Robert Sietsema, Matt Konigsmark, Judith Fertig, Jane Snow, John Long, Bill Addison, Reagan Walker, Christiane Lauterbach, and the desk clerk at the Avalon who helped me plot the thirty-seven stops on my Los Angeles trip. And then there's Brett Anderson, Pete Wells, Susan Choi, Ed Levine, Bill Summers, Ted Lee, Matt Lee, Emily Winkey, Sarah Fritschner, Michael Griffith, Bob Yeats, Carol Daily, Viviana Carbollo, Kathleen Purvis, and Barbara Kuck of the Culinary Archives & Museum at Johnson & Wales University. And let's not forget my colleagues at the Southern Foodways Alliance, or Mary Beth Lasseter, Mary Hartwell Howorth, Charles Wilson, Ann Abadie, and my colleagues at the Center for the Study of Southern Culture.

About the Author

John T. Edge writes for *Gourmet, Saveur,* and other publications. His work was featured in the 2001 through 2004 editions of the *Best Food Writing* compilation. Edge has a number of books to his credit, including the James Beard Award–nominated cookbook *A Gracious Plenty: Recipes and Recollections from the American South.* He is a finalist for the 2004 M. F. K. Fisher Distinguished Writing Award from the James Beard Foundation.

Edge holds a master's degree in Southern Studies and is director of the Southern Foodways Alliance, an institute of the Center for the Study of Southern Culture at the University of Mississippi, where he dedicates his time to studying, celebrating, promoting, and preserving America's diverse food cultures.

He is one of the founders and principals of the Civil Rights Commemoration Initiative, which is working to install a memorial to the civil rights movement at the University of Mississippi. In 2003, he was named "One of Twenty Southerners to Watch" by the *Financial Times* of London. The recognition singles out people "whose achievements will have a greater impact in the future, both on the national and international stage."

Edge lives in Oxford, Mississippi, with his son, Jesse, and his wife, Blair Hobbs, a painter. Visit the author's website at www.johntedge.com.